D0115961

BROOKDALE
Jr. High School
Library

BOOKS BY CHARLES F. LINN

PUZZLES, PATTERNS, AND PASTIMES
ODD ANGLES
ESTIMATION

ODD ANGLES

ODD ANGLES

THIRTY-THREE MATHEMATICAL ENTERTAINMENTS

CHARLES F. LINN

DOUBLEDAY & COMPANY, INC., GARDEN CITY, NEW YORK

1971

510
LINN

BROOKDALE JUNIOR HIGH SCHOOL
1415 EAST HEATON LAKE ROAD
ELKHART, INDIANA   46514

Library of Congress Catalogue Card Number 70–116228
Copyright © 1971 by Charles F. Linn
All Rights Reserved
Printed in the United States of America

Grateful acknowledgment is made for the use of the following copyrighted material:

"How to Estimate Distance" from LET THE CRABGRASS GROW by H. Allen Smith, copyright 1948, 1960. Reprinted by permission of Harold Matson Company, Inc.

"Arithmetic" by Carl Sandburg. Copyright 1950, by Carl Sandburg. Reprinted from his volume COMPLETE POEMS by permission of Harcourt, Brace & World, Inc.

"Mathematics Versus Puzzles" by Stephen L. Leacock, reprinted by permission of Dodd, Mead & Company, Inc., from TOO MUCH COLLEGE by Stephen Leacock. Copyright 1939 by Dodd, Mead and Company, Inc. Copyright renewed 1967 by Stephen L. Leacock.

"Why Parents Can't Add" by Art Buchwald, reprinted by permission of G. P. Putnam's Sons from SON OF THE GREAT SOCIETY by Art Buchwald. Copyright © 1965, 1966 by Art Buchwald.

"February 28" "April 11" "April 17" "May 18" "July 1" "July 12" and "December 25," by Will Cuppy. From HOW TO GET FROM JANUARY TO DECEMBER by Will Cuppy, edited by Fred Feldkamp. Copyright 1951 by Fred Feldkamp. Reprinted by permission of Holt, Rinehart and Winston, Inc.

"Euclid" by Vachel Lindsay. Reprinted with permission of The Macmillan Company from COLLECTED POEMS by Vachel Lindsay. Copyright 1914 by The Macmillan Company, renewed 1942 by Elizabeth C. Lindsay.

"The Feeling of Power" by Isaac Asimov, by permission of Dr. Asimov.
"The Wise Man of Sumatra" by David Eugene Smith, by permission of
Scripta Mathematica.
"Carl Friedrich Ruins the Schoolmaster's Nap" by Robert A. Rosenbaum
by permission of Dr. Rosenbaum.
"A Pure Mathematician" by Arthur Guiterman. Reprinted by permission
from Mrs. Arthur Guiterman.
"Agha and Math" by Vladimir Karapatoff. Reprinted by permission of
Scripta Mathematica.
"Vision" by George David Birkhoff. Reprinted by permission of Harvard
University Press. Copyright 1933 by the President and Fellows of Harvard
College; 1961 by Garrett Birkhoff.
An untitled poem from Ireland by William Rowan Hamilton. Reprinted
by permission of *Scripta Mathematica.*
The excerpt described as "Numbers Are Wonderful Things" by Thomas
Mann, from THE YOUNG JOSEPH. With permission of Alfred A. Knopf, Inc.
Copyright 1935 by Alfred A. Knopf.
"With Words a Bit Garbled" from THE CHRISTMAS THAT ALMOST
WASN'T by Ogden Nash, by permission of Little, Brown and Company.
Copyright © 1957 by Ogden Nash.
"Parabola" by Hooper Reynolds Goodwin. Reprinted by permission of
the Manchester (New Hampshire) *Union Leader.*

For the members of the Math 16.03 section
in the fall semester, 1968, at Oswego State College,
in particular
. . . and for the mathematically disinclined
(and disenchanted), in general.

CONTENTS

CONTENTS

MATHEMATICIANS IN STRANGE PLACES

IT'S STRANGE MATHEMATICS, IN PLACES

INTRODUCTION

Many people seem to be convinced that mathematicians are strange characters who stand around and mumble numbers to themselves, or, at best, to other mathematicians. And, they also think that mathematics is strange stuff reserved exclusively for these mathematicians. Thus you have even Carl Sandburg saying

> Arithmetic is numbers you squeeze from your head
> to your hand
> to your pencil
> to your paper
> till you get the right answer.

and things like that.

But, I feel very strongly that mathematics is something which everyone can do at least a bit of. And that mathematicians are people too—at least, in the same proportions as is the public in general.

I hope the selections in this book will help to prove my case.

Now, I would find it quite astonishing (and even a little scary) if everyone became convinced to the point of agreeing with the poet who wrote that

There is something beautiful about Math
And the people who love it
It provides an anchor in a restless sea
And while all about, the waves of passion and unrest break
Mathematics is so firm and solid . . .

I'll settle for a concession that "math can be kind of fun,
after all."

Charles Linn
Turkey Hill
1970

STRANGERS
IN
MATHEMATICAL PLACES

1

HOW TO ESTIMATE DISTANCE
H. ALLEN SMITH

Estimation is serious business. At least you would think so when you hear math teachers talk about it, and lament of how poorly their students do at it. I've contributed a lamentation here and there myself.

Perhaps, then we should look for a fresh approach to the subject and consult a non-math type with a bent for the practical. If you don't do so well at estimating, this excerpt from H. Allen Smith's book *Let the Crabgrass Grow* may be just what you are looking for.

And, if the book title indicates that Mr. Smith may not be taking this serious business seriously enough, consider a few other titles of books he has written . . .

Low Man on a Totem Pole
Life in a Putty Knife Factory
Larks in the Popcorn
The Pig in the Barber Shop
Write Me a Poem, Baby

On the theory that other people have trouble estimating distances I have worked out a small table of helpful suggestions.

THREE FEET: If you are of average height you may be surprised to learn that your leg is just about three feet, or one

3

yard, long. So if you need to estimate three feet, kick your leg straight out in front of you and hold it there and look at it.

NINE FEET: Not long ago in Honolulu I met the proprietor of a cemetery (I met him socially) and for some reason we got to talking about distances and he said he was very good at nine feet, which is the required length of a grave in Hawaii. He said it is ten feet on the mainland.

TEN FEET: See nine feet.

THIRTEEN FEET: Think of two Gary Coopers lying end to end, both wearing cowboy boots. This same system can be used in estimating six and a half feet, with only one Cooper.

FIFTEEN FEET: At the age of five I fell into a freshly dug cistern and I can remember that everyone made a big thing out of the fact that it was "fifteen-foot" deep. That distance is ineradicably and traumatically engraved on my mind. The trouble is, however, it is a vertical distance and somehow I can't seem to bend it over and flatten it out against the ground. It will come in handy, however, if I am ever fifteen feet up a telegraph pole and want to notify people how far up a telegraph pole I am.

TWENTY-FIVE FEET: I always get my wife to estimate this one for me. It is the precise distance the man skidded before crashing into her car that day on the Saw Mill River Parkway. The police measured the skid marks and she says she now knows twenty-five feet better than she knows her own children. If you happen to witness an automobile accident in which someone has skidded, worm your way in close and observe the measurement of the tire marks. It's better, of course, to be *in* the accident.

SEVENTEEN FEET: Measure the over-all length of your automobile. It may turn out to be seventeen feet. Memorize that length by walking from bumper to bumper, back and forth, reciting over and over, "Seventeen feet, seventeen feet, seventeen feet." Don't be embarrassed if a neighbor comes along and catches you at it. Simply tell him that you are rehearsing a part in an amateur theatrical production, a detective story.

SIXTY FEET: Recently the skipper of an auxiliary ketch asked me to sign on as a member of his crew and sail with him to Tahiti. I wanted to do it and spent an entire afternoon pacing that little vessel from stem to stern, trying to make up my mind. I compared its size to that of a huge ocean liner that had recently docked with a cargo of seasick passengers and shattered furniture. I learned sixty feet so well that I'll always know it but as far as the Tahitian voyage was concerned, I chickened out. A full-grown chicken is eleven inches long, if you want to remember eleven inches.

NINETEEN MILES: It is a good thing to know this distance in case there is a town or a tavern nineteen miles from where you live, and you want to tell your neighbors how far they'll have to go to get there. The best way to learn to estimate nineteen miles is to grease up and swim the English Channel. An easier method is to go to that tavern.

NINETY-THREE MILLION MILES: We now have all kinds of astronomical distances to worry about from day to day, and we might as well try to cope with them. It's almost frightening to realize that the moonshooters, employing the technique of a hunter leading a duck, aim their rockets at a point about 137,000 miles ahead of their moving target. I heard a man say so. Now there is talk of shooting something at the sun. The mean distance from the earth to the sun is 93,000,000 miles. That's a mean distance to estimate, but it can be done. The moon is only 239,000 miles from the earth and we have come to know that distance pretty intimately. Thus it becomes a simple matter to visualize the distance from Cape Kennedy to the sun. The way it figures out, it is 390 times as far to the sun as it is to the moon. Get the moon distance (239,000 miles, give or take a yard) firmly fixed in your mind and then lay it out 390 times (the way I do it with football fields) and when you've got it laid out end to end 390 times, you'll have the distance to the sun just as solidly fixed in your mind. That is, *you'll* have it. I don't think I will, because I'm going back to the old-fashioned ways, back to that bird on the stump.

2

ARITHMETIC

CARL SANDBURG

Arithmetic is where numbers fly like pigeons in and out of
your head.

Arithmetic tells you how many you lose or win if you know
how many you had before you lost or won.

Arithmetic is seven eleven all good children go to heaven
—or five six bundle of sticks.

Arithmetic is numbers you squeeze from your head to your
hand to your pencil to your paper till you get the answer.

Arithmetic is where the answer is right and everything is
nice and you can look out of the window and see the blue
sky—or the answer is wrong and you have to start all
over and try again and see how it comes out this time.

If you take a number and double it and double it again
and then double it a few more times, the number gets
bigger and bigger and goes higher and higher and only
arithmetic can tell you what the number is when you
decide to quit doubling.

Arithmetic is where you have to multiply—and you carry
the multiplication table in your head and hope you won't
lose it.

If you have two animal crackers, one good and one bad,
and you eat one and a striped zebra with streaks all over
him eats the other, how many animal crackers will you
have if somebody offers you five six seven and you say

7

No no no and you say Nay nay nay and you say Nix
nix nix?

If you ask your mother for one fried egg for breakfast and
she gives you two fried eggs and you eat both of them,
who is better in arithmetic, you or your mother?

THE MOST MAGICALLY MAGICAL

BENJAMIN FRANKLIN

I'll include here a copy of a letter from Benjamin Franklin to Peter Collinson, in London. He describes the properties of his magic square of order sixteen, which he calls "the most magically magical of any magic square ever made by any magician."
And, that's some magic.

Sir,
According to your request I now send you the arithmetical curiosity, of which this is the history.

Being one day in the country, at the house of our common friend, the late learned Mr. Logan, he showed me a folio French book filled with magic squares, wrote, if I forget not, by one M. Frenicle, in which he said the author had discovered great ingenuity and dexterity in the management of numbers; and though several other foreigners had distinguished themselves in the same way, he did not recollect that any one Englishman had done any thing of the kind remarkable.

I said, it was, perhaps, a mark of the good sense of our English mathematicians, that they would not spend their time in things that were merely *difficiles nugæ*, incapable of any useful application. He answered, that many of the arithmetical or mathematical questions, publicly proposed and answered in England, were equally trifling and useless. Perhaps the considering and answering such questions, I replied, may not be altogether useless, if it produces by practice an habitual readiness and exactness in mathematical disquisitions, which readiness may, on many occasions, be of real use. In the same way, says he, may the making of these squares be of use. I then confessed to him, that in my younger days, having once some leisure (which I still think I might have employed more usefully) I had amused myself in making these kind of magic squares, and, at length, had acquired such a knack at it, that I could fill the cells of any magic square of reasonable size, with a series of numbers as fast as I could write them, disposed in such a manner as that the sums of every row, horizontal, perpendicular, or diagonal, should be equal; but not being satisfied with these, which I looked on as common and easy things, I had imposed on myself more difficult tasks, and succeeded in making other magic squares, with a variety of properties, and much more curious. He then shewed me several in the same book, of an uncommon and more curious kind; but as I thought none of them equal to some I remembered to have made, he desired me to let him see them; and accordingly, the next time I visited him, I carried him a square of 8, which I found among my old papers, and which I will now give you, with an account of its properties.

The properties are,

1. That every strait row (horizontal or vertical) of 8 numbers added together makes 260, and half each row half 260.

2. That the bent row of 8 numbers, ascending and de-

A Magic Square of Squares.

200	217	232	249	8	25	40	57	72	89	104	121	136	153	168	181
58	39	26	7	250	231	218	199	186	167	154	135	122	103	90	71
198	219	230	251	6	27	38	59	70	91	102	123	134	155	166	187
60	37	28	5	252	229	220	197	188	165	156	133	124	101	92	69
201	216	233	248	9	24	41	56	73	88	105	120	137	152	169	184
55	42	23	10	247	234	215	202	183	170	151	138	119	106	87	74
20	214	235	246	11	22	43	54	75	86	107	118	139	150	171	182
56	44	21	12	245	236	213	204	181	172	149	140	117	108	85	76
205	212	237	244	13	20	45	52	77	84	109	116	141	148	173	180
51	46	19	14	243	238	241	206	179	174	147	142	115	110	83	78
207	210	239	242	15	18	47	50	79	82	111	114	143	146	175	178
49	48	17	16	241	240	209	208	177	176	145	144	113	112	81	80
196	221	228	253	4	29	36	61	68	93	100	125	132	157	164	189
62	35	30	3	254	227	222	195	190	163	158	131	126	99	94	67
194	223	226	255	2	31	34	63	66	95	98	127	130	159	162	191
64	33	32	1	256	225	224	193	192	161	160	129	128	97	96	65

scending diagonally, viz. from 16 ascending to 10, and from 23 descending to 17; and every one of its parallel bent rows of 8 numbers make 260.—Also the bent row from 52 descending to 54, and from 43 ascending to 45; and every one of its parallel bent rows of 8 numbers make 260.—Also the bent row from 45 to 43, descending to the left, and from 23 to 17, descending to the right, and every one of its

11

parallel bent rows of 8 numbers, make 260.—Also the bent row from 52 to 54, descending to the right, and from 10 to 16, descending to the left, and every one of its parallel bent rows of 8 numbers make 260.—Also the parallel bent rows next to the above-mentioned, which are shortened to 3 numbers ascending, and 3 descending, &c. as from 53 to 4 ascending, and from 29 to 44 descending, make, with the two corner numbers, 260.—Also the 3 numbers 14, 61 ascending, and 36, 19 descending, with the lower 4 numbers situated like them, viz. 50, 1, descending, and 32, 47, ascending, make 260.—And, lastly, the 4 corner numbers, with the 4 middle numbers, make 260.

So this magical square seems perfect in its kind. But these are not all its properties; there are 5 other curious ones, which, at some other time, I will explain to you.

Mr. Logan then shewed me an old arithmetical book, in quarto, wrote, I think, by one Stifelius, which contained a square of 16, that he said he should imagine must have been a work of great labour; but if I forget not, it had only the common properties of making the same sum, viz. 2056, in every row, horizontal, vertical, and diagonal. Not willing to be out-done by Mr. Stifelius, even in the size of my square, I went home, and made, that evening, the following magical square of 16, which, besides having all the properties of the foregoing square of 8, i. e. it would make the 2056 in all the same rows and diagonals, had this added, that a four-square hole being cut in a piece of paper of such a size as to take in and show through it just 16 of the little squares, when laid on the greater square, the sum of the 16 numbers so appearing through the hole, wherever it was placed on the greater square, should likewise make 2056. This I sent to our friend the next morning, who, after some days, sent it back in a letter with these words: "I return to thee thy astonishing or most stupendous piece of the magical square, in which—" but the compliment is too extravagant, and therefore, for his sake, as well as my own, I ought not to repeat it. Nor is it necessary; for I make no question but you will readily allow this square of 16 to be the most magically magical of any magic square ever made by any magician. (*See the Plate.*)

I did not, however, end with squares, but composed also a magic circle, consisting of 8 concentric circles, and 8 radial rows, filled with a series of numbers from 12 to 75 inclusive, so disposed as that the numbers of each circle, or each radial row, being added to the central number 12, they make exactly 360, the number of degrees in a circle; and this circle had, moreover, all the properties of the square of 8. If you desire it, I will send it; but at present, I believe, you have enough on this subject. I am, &c.

B. FRANKLIN.

4

MATHEMATICS VERSUS PUZZLES
STEPHEN LEACOCK

Stephen Leacock was not really typical of those people who claim to be "non-math types." At least I have found that many such folk enjoy a mathematical puzzle or game and want no part of "mathematics." However, I agree with him on some of the examples he cites in this essay, for their solutions depend on tricks, rather than mathematics.

Mr. Leacock was for many years professor of English at McGill University and recognized as a scholar in academic circles. He is best known, however, for his humorous writings. At that, there may be more than a little seriousness in the title of the book from which this essay comes, *Too Much College*.

Before getting on with "Mathematics Versus Puzzles," I would like to insert one of my favorite quotes—Stephen Leacock's characterization of statistics:

"In earlier times they had no statistics and so they had to fall back on lies. Hence the huge exaggerations of primitive literature—giants or miracles or wonders! They did it with lies and we do it with statistics, but it is all the same."

I remember being taken as a boy of twelve years old to listen to a "paper" at the University of Toronto Literary

14

and Debating Society, on the question, "Are mathematical judgments synthetically *a priori?*" In those simple days before "pictures" and radio and motor-cars and emancipated girls, to go and listen to a "paper" or to a debate between two black-robed students, sipping water off a table, was presumed to be first-class fun. When they discussed mathematical judgments and whether or not *a priori,* I felt that I didn't understand it, but that I would when I grew up. That's where I was wrong.

I am still very vague as to what mathematical judgments being synthetically *a priori* means. I imagine it refers to the question how do we know that one and one makes two, and if it does, what do we mean by it? But at any rate it bears witness to the profundity of mathematics—I mean, its reach toward the infinite and the unknowable.

This element of fundamental mystery has been expanded in our own day by the glorious confusion introduced by Professor Einstein into all our notions of distance, time and magnitude. How far is one thing from another? The question becomes unknowable. It may be twice as far away as something else is, or half as far; but, beyond the relative number, there seems no such thing as solid distance. What is a foot? Twelve inches. What is an inch? One twelfth of a foot. Similarly where is *here?* And when is *now?*

I only refer to these mysteries in order to explain why I still have to speak of mathematics in a reverential whisper, like a Christian entering a Mohammedan mosque, in wicker slippers. He knows it's a revered place though he doesn't understand it.

My attitude toward mathematics, indeed, is that of nine out of ten of educated people—a sense of awe, something like horror, a gratitude for escape but at times a wistful feeling of regret, a sense that there might have been more made of it. Everything, therefore, that I say about mathematics is tempered by so great a humility as to rob it of all controversial aspect. But I do think that as far as a practical school curriculum goes I could shorten it by at least one half. What I would do, to express it in a single phrase, would be to separate true mathematics from mathematical puzzles.

If mathematics is for many students the dragon in the path, these puzzles are the dragon's teeth. Take them out and the dragon is as easy to handle as a cow. Children learn to count and add and multiply, and feel that it is all plain and straightforward; the multiplication table may be tricky, but it's fair. Then presently comes a "puzzle" problem. "What number," says the teacher to the child, "is made up of two figures, the second meaning twice as many as the first, and the two adding up to nine?"

Now, this is not mathematics in the proper sense; this is a puzzle. The only true mathematical operation here would be to set down all the numbers of two digits, from 10 to 99 in turn, and see which one fitted it. But when it comes to guessing and choosing, to ingenuity, that's a puzzle. Half our school mathematics in algebra and geometry consist of "puzzles," freak equations and inventive geometry. Students are not discoverers. Pythagoras solved the problem of the squares on the right-angled triangle. I'm willing to "take it as read" and learn it in ten minutes.

This puzzle "bunker" is built right across the mathematical fairway and down the middle of it. "Scholars" pound the sand in it and wonder why they can't do mathematics. True mathematics means a process learned and used; hard to learn, but later, second nature. Show me how to extract a square root and I'll extract it as neatly as a dentist. Tell a ship's captain how to calculate the angle of the sun's declination and show a broker's clerk how to use logarithms for compound interest. But don't expect a student to be a discoverer, working out "problems" which Isaac Newton or Copernicus might solve or miss.

Now at the present time all schoolbooks on mathematics are mixtures of what may be called "sums," "problems" and "mathematical puzzles." A sum is an operation dealing with numbers and following a definite and known routine of calculation. When a waiter adds up a restaurant check he performs a sum. A calculating machine can do a sum. But it can't do a problem. For a problem is an operation involving a selection of methods of calculation, of which only certain ones will fit the case. A schoolboy calculating when the hour hand of a clock will overtake the minute hand is working out a problem. There are plenty of wrong ways of working at it, as when Achilles tried to overtake a tortoise, and kept the Greeks guessing for generations. But the schoolboy soon finds that there are a whole lot of problems dealing with motion and time which all fall into a definite and known method of solution that becomes itself as familiar as the waiter's addition table. Now the extension of a problem in difficulty and intricacy, to where only one method of many will bring a solution, turns it, at some point, into a puzzle.

When Archimedes jumped out of his bath and shouted "Eureka," what he had solved was not a problem but a puzzle. He had been asked by some king or other, had he not? how to tell whether a gold crown was really a gold crown or was made of two metals melted together. A modern chemist would find this out with an acid. But Archimedes found a way without chemistry. Yet a professor of mathematics might take a bath every morning for years and never think of it. Since there was no way of forcing a solution by an inevitable method, the thing was not a problem but a puzzle.

Such a puzzle is legitimate enough, though it is no true test of mathematical knowledge. But further out on the field are puzzles that may be called illegitimate, since they present the added difficulty of misleading or paradoxical language. For the information and perhaps the diversion of the reader, let me illustrate the difference. Here is a legitimate puzzle. A man wishes to buy a piece of linoleum that is to cover a space 12 feet by 12. A dealer offers him a piece that is 9 feet by 16 feet. Obviously each piece contains 144 square feet. The dealer tells the customer that all he needs to do is to cut the piece that is 9 feet by 16 feet into two separate pieces that can then be fitted together to cover 12 feet by 12 feet. This of course—or rather *not* of course, for few people can do it—is done by drawing lines across the 12 by 12 piece, 3 feet apart in one direction and 4 feet in the other. Start 9 feet east from the top northwest corner and cut along the lines alternately south and west, and there you are. But such a puzzle does not belong in mathematical education although it corresponds in nature to a lot of the things called "problems" that wreck the lives of students.

Here however is a sample of an illegitimate puzzle. A man has 17 camels. He leaves them in his will to his three sons, ½ to the eldest, ⅓ to the next and ⅑ to the youngest. But these fractions won't divide unless you cut up the camels themselves. When the sons are still in perplexity a dervish happens to pass by, riding on a camel. Dervishes

18

always ride by on camels at convenient moments in these
Arabian problems. The sons tell him of their dilemma.
After deep thought—dervishes always think deeply—he says,
"Let me lend you my camel to make eighteen instead of
seventeen. Now take one half which is nine, and one third
which is six, and one ninth which is two, and you each have
your proper share. And as *nine* and *six* and *two* only add
up to seventeen, you may kindly return my camel." With
which the dervish departed, and the sons no doubt told the
story all the rest of their lives.

Now this problem is of course as full of fallacies as a
sieve is full of holes. In the first place the sons didn't
get ½ and ⅓ and ⅑ of 17 but of something else: and when
the father left them these fractions, a little arithmetic—
beyond them, no doubt—would have shown that ½ and ⅓
and ⅑ of a thing don't add up to the whole thing but only
to $^{17}/_{18}$ of it. There was still $^{1}/_{18}$ of each camel coming to
somebody.

Here is another type of puzzle problem turning on misleading suggestion. Three men at a summer hotel were
going fishing and were told they must pay 10 dollars each
for a license. They each put up 10 dollars and sent it by a
hotel boy to the inspector's office. The boy came back with
5 dollars and said that the inspector had made a rebate of
5 dollars out of 30, because it was understood they were
all one party in the same boat. The men, greatly pleased,
gave the boy 2 dollars out of the 5 and kept one each. One
of them then said: "Look here! This is odd. We expected our
fishing to cost ten dollars each (thirty dollars) and it has
only cost us nine dollars each, and two to the boy. Three
times nine is twenty-seven, and two makes twenty-nine;
where has the other dollar of the thirty gone?"

The reader no doubt sees the fallacy instantly; but some people wouldn't.

Now I admit that textbooks on mathematics never push the problems quite as far as this on illegitimate puzzle ground—unless indeed they do it on purpose, as in the book of *Mathematical Recreations* once compiled by the celebrated Professor Ball. But what I claim is that the element of the problem, and even of the puzzle, looms far too large in mathematics as we have it. Indeed for most people it overshadows the subject and ends their advance.

The ordinary straight "discipline" of school mathematics should consist of plain methods of calculation, like division, square root, highest common factor and so on, or such problems as conform to a recognized method of regular solution. All that goes in arithmetic under the name of the "unitary method" is of this class. If A in one hour can do twice as much work as B does in two hours, then—well, we know all about them. Yet few people realize that this beautiful and logical unitary method is quite new—I mean belongs only in the last two generations. When I first learned arithmetic it was just emerging from the "rule-of-three" in the dim light of which all such calculations appeared something like puzzles.

In algebra also a vast part of the subject can be studied as regular calculation, or at least as a problem of regular order, such as the motion and time illustration mentioned above. I gather, also, that another large section of algebraical calculation, though capable of being effected by short, ingenious, or individual methods, can always, if need be, be submitted to a forced operation, clumsy but inevitable— as if a person wanting to know how many squares there are on a chessboard counted them one by one.

To illustrate what I mean, let me call back, from nearly sixty years ago, the recollection of our Sixth Form class in mathematics at Upper Canada College. Our master, Mr. Brown, was a mathematician, the real thing, with a gold medal in proof of it, and gold spectacles through which he saw little but x and y—gentle, simple and out of the world. The class had early discovered that Mr. Brown, with a long equation on the blackboard and his back to the class, would stay there indefinitely, in his academic cap and gown, lost in a reverie in which the bonds of discipline fell apart. So the thing was to supply him with a sufficiently tough equation.

This became the special business of the *farceur* of the class, a large and cheerful joker called Donald Armour, later on the staff of the Rush Medical College and a distinguished Harley Street surgeon. Armour would approach Mr. Brown in the morning and say, "I was looking over some Woolwich examination papers last night, Mr. Brown, and I found this equation. I can't make anything of it." "Oh!" said Mr. Brown with interest. He accepted without question the idea that Armour spent his evenings in mathematics. "Let me look at it, Armour." Then another spirit in collusion would call out, "Won't you put it on the board, Mr. Brown?" And in a minute there it was, strung out along the blackboard, a tangled mass of x's and y's and squares and cubes, with Mr. Brown in front of it, as still as Rodin's *penseur*.

Meanwhile the class relaxed into easy conversation, and Armour threw paper darts with pins in the end to try and hit Mr. Brown in the yoke of his gown. Presently, without turning round, Mr. Brown spoke. "Of course, I could *force* it . . ."

"Oh, please, Mr. Brown," pleaded Armour, "don't force it!" and there came a chorus from the class, "Don't force it, Mr. Brown," and subdued laughter, because we didn't know what forcing it was, anyway. "I assure you, gentlemen, I shall not force it until I have tried every expedient." A chorus of thanks and a renewed reverie. Then presently Mr. Brown would suddenly turn toward us and say excitedly:

"Did you try a function of m, Armour?"

"I never thought of it."

"It may resolve it." And away rattled Mr. Brown's chalk, line upon line, till there stretched the equation, solved! To us it looked bigger than ever.

I won't swear that it was a function of m that did the trick. It may have been one of the other mystic agents such as a "coefficient of x," or perhaps pi, a household word to us, as vague as it was familiar.

But what I mean is that when Mr. Brown said he could "force" an equation he referred to a definite mathematical process, as certain as extracting a square root and needing only time and patience.

What I am saying, then, is that school mathematics, and college mathematics as far as made compulsory, should be made up in great proportion, in overwhelming proportion, of straight calculation. I admit that the element of ingenuity, of individual discovery, must also count for something; but for most people even the plainest of plain calculations contain something of it. For many people the multiplication table is still full of happy surprises: and a person not mathematical but trained to calculate compound interest with a logarithm can get as much fun out of it as Galileo could with the moon.

Now to many people, mathematicians by nature, all that I have said about problems and puzzles is merely a revelation of ignorance. These things, they say, are the essence of mathematics. The rest of it is as wooden as a Chinese abacus. They would tell me that I am substituting a calculating machine for a calculating mind. I admit it, in a degree. But the reason for it is perhaps that that is all most of us are capable of. We have not been made "mathematically minded," and hence the failure of our mathematics.

I am of course stepping out here on gound where wiser feet might hesitate to tread. But I think that for most of us something goes wrong, very early in school, with our mathematical sense, our mathematical conceptions— or rather with the conceptions that we fail to get. We get lost in the symbols of mathematics and can't visualize the realities—visualize or dramatize, or whatever you do with them. Mathematics is always, for most of us, a sort of mystery which we don't even expect to understand. Let me illustrate the attitude by recalling a joke of a stage "review" of a few years ago. Some boys are seen coming out of school, comically overgrown and comically underdressed, grown too long and dressed too short, so as to make them look funny.

"Well, my little man," says a stock stage gentleman, in the stock voice of a stage question, "and what are you learning at school?"

"Reading and writing," says one of the comedian boys, his immobile face a marvel of wooden imbecility, blank as the alphabet.

"Reading and writing," repeats the stock gentleman, so as to let the audience get it, "and anything else?"

The "boy" answers, with no facial movement, "We learn gazinta."

"You learn what?"

"Gazinta."

"But what is gazinta?"

"Why," explains the boy, "like 'two gazinta four' and 'five gazinta ten.'"

The roar of the audience's laughter ends the mathematics. They laugh because in the contrast between the clarity of reading and writing and the mystery of "gazinta" they see their own experience. For them all mathematics is, and always will be, "gazinta."

Here is a particular example, familiar to all school and college people, of what I mean by our failure to get a proper grasp of mathematical thought. We all learn that the attraction of gravity exercised on or by a body varies in direct proportion to its mass, and inversely as the square of its distance. The square? That's the sticker for most of us. What's the square got to do with it? We understand, or we think we do, that of course the more "mass" a thing has the more it pulls. In reality this is the real philosophical difficulty, since mass means power to "pull," and "pull" means having mass. But we don't look into it so far as that; the bigger the mass, the bigger the pull, all right. But the square of the distance we accept, learn it by heart, use it, multiply it—in short, it becomes "gazinta." It seems an odd thing. Why the square? Why not the cube, or the anything else? We don't see, till we learn to get it straight, that the thing is self-evident.

The pull varies with the amount of *surface*, a thing of two dimensions, broad and long. A tower at a certain distance (don't call it x or we'll get mixed) looks a certain height and looks a certain breadth. A tower twice as far away would have to be twice as high to look level with it and twice as broad to look of the same breadth. So the far-away tower at twice the distance of the near one, in order to look the same size, would have to be twice as high and twice as broad and would present to the eye four square feet to one, in order to present an apparently equal surface. The attraction is in proportion to the surface and gets less and less for any given size of surface as you go further away. And it doesn't matter if the surface is square or round or triangular, or any other shape, since they are all proportional. Here I believe is where *pi* comes in—but don't let us go too far with it.

There are ever so many of these mathematical conceptions that turned into mystification because we never got them right at the start. The trigonometrical ratios—sine, cosine, etc.—seemed just an arbitrary iniquity. If we had thought of them as moving arms, like traffic signs, we would have felt them to be the natural and inevitable way of measuring an angle.

It seems to me, therefore, that something might be done, at the very opening of education, to strengthen our grip on the mathematical idea. This would bring us back, I presume, to those mathematical judgments synthetically *a priori* with which I started. The question involved is the nature of number and magnitude, and why does one and one make two? and the consideration whether a statement of that sort is just a fact or an inference from one judgment to another. I imagine that if we could see into one another's minds we should find a great difference in our grasp on the sequence of numbers. A hen, it is understood, can distinguish two from one but is lost at three. Primitive languages count a little way and then say "a whole lot." Here figures end and lies begin. Even the Greeks used to say "a myriad" to mean not an exact number but ever so many.

We have fallen heirs to the wonderful ingenuity of what we call Arabic notation. In reality the Hindus started it, but the Arabs made it plainer still by writing into it a "cipher" or "zero" to mark a blank place. We learn it so early in life and so artificially that we don't appreciate it. We think of ten as an arbitrary point, whereas the shift to a new "place" could have been set anywhere, and would be better if set at something more divisible than ten. If the people on Mars have brains as much better than ours as their planet is older, they may use a set of numbers that would go thousands at a jump and write the population of the United States in three figures. We couldn't of course do that. The multiplication table used for it would be beyond our learning. But I am sure that we, the non-mathematical people among whom I belong, would get a better grip on mathematics if we had a better conception of the relationship of numbers and symbols.

I am aware of course that there are many recent books that attempt to shed new light on mathematics. But the light seems dim. One or two well-known "series" contain what are really admirable presentations of the philosophy of mathematics. But, for the ordinary person, to mix philosophy with mathematics only makes it worse. Other popular works undertake to bring mathemetics to the intelligence of the millions; it would be invidious to name the books, but, apart from their optimistic titles, I cannot see much success in them.

I am aware also that various new methods of teaching

mathematics are adopted, especially in teaching mathematics to beginners. But in any that I have seen there is little else than one more example of the present tendency to turn children's education into fun. Kindergarten children waving little flags, forming themselves into squares and cubes and separating themselves into fractions, may look very pretty, but they are no nearer to the mysteries of number. Singing the multiplication table doesn't make it less relentless.

Here on my desk, for instance, is a widely known pretentious book of "new method." It undertakes to "individualize arithmetic" by teaching the children what the author calls "number facts" by the use of numbered cards. "Cards," says this authority, "are invaluable for learning number facts." Many of us found this out long ago. The children "individualize" their arithmetic by sitting in a ring, dealing out cards with numbers and pictures on them, and then seeing whose "number facts" win out against their opponents. The children might learn poker from this but not mathematics. What they are doing sounds like a "showdown" of "cold hands," a process as old as California.

The basic idea of my discussion is that somehow we don't get our minds mathematically adjusted as they might be. I am aware that there are great differences of natural aptitude. We are told that Isaac Newton when he was a boy took a look through Euclid's *Elements* and said it seemed a "trifling book." That meant that, when Euclid said, "the three angles of a triangle are together equal to two right angles," little Newton said, "Why, of course, obviously so." Probably the Pythagorean theorum about the squares on the sides of a right-angled triangle only held him back a minute or two. These things took the rest of us a year of school. But, all said and done, I think that it is not only a matter of aptitude but of approach. We don't "go at it" right.

With that I leave the subject, with the hopes that at least it may be stimulating to professors of mathematics. A little stimulant won't hurt them.

5

THE MULTIPLICATION TABLE
MARK TWAIN

I got as far as six times
seven is thirty-five and
I don't guess I'll need any
more than that.
       . . . Huck Finn

6

AN UNSUCCESSFUL FRENCH GENERAL
CHARLES F. LINN

I am quite convinced that if you wait long enough and look around carefully enough you will find that most everyone will show up on the mathematical scene. Certainly one of the least likely candidates was Charles Denis Sauter Bourbaki, a nineteenth-century French general—and a very unsuccessful one at that.

Bourbaki apparently spent some time in the city of Nancy, France, for it is said that a statue of him once stood there. He was soundly defeated by the Germans in the Franco-Prussian War, and retreated to Switzerland with the remnants of his forces. There they were interned for the duration. Bourbaki was so distressed over his failure that he twice tried to commit suicide. Surviving both efforts, he eventually returned to civilian life, ran for the Chamber of Deputies twice, and was defeated both times. He eventually expired at the age of eighty-one.

Now, why a group of mathematicians would take the Bourbaki name for their collective pseudonym is a great mystery to one and all. But, since 1939 "Nicholas Bourbaki" has been publishing very high-level and very important mathematical works. Identities of the individual mathematicians are kept secret, but the group and the publisher have worked hard at making up a biography for Bourbaki.

The publisher, Enrique Freymann, even went a bit overboard: "Beware of killing a phantom," he said to an over-eager reporter. "Bourbaki is nowhere and everywhere. And you want to tame him, to trap him. What madness! One must not limit universality. We had to create a new man in harmony with the new mankind, something between human being and cybernetics. That new man is Bourbaki. If civilization is to survive, it needs a creature who thirsts only for knowledge and never dies. Such is Bourbaki. Man survives through Bourbaki, the supreme creation of modern man."

That miserable general has come a long way.

Since 1939 we have found out quite a bit about this secret society. Among other things, the society is made up of about eighteen or twenty mathematicians, and the membership changes from time to time, for these people are convinced that mathematics is a young man's "game." A member must retire at the age of forty-five, and earlier, if, through a process known as shaking the coconut tree, members decide that another member no longer is as sharp, mathematically, as he should be.

"Shaking the coconut tree" comes from a custom of the South Sea island people who, when they suspected that a chief was no longer capable of ruling, would make him climb a coconut tree. Then the other men in the tribe would shake the tree. If the chief held on, he was fit to continue to rule. But, if he did not hold on . . . well, new chief.

The Bourbaki people do not make the suspect member climb a tree. The other members merely fire complicated mathematical questions at him. If he holds his own, he continues in the society. But if this shaking is more than he can handle . . . the others look for a new member.

7

WHY PARENTS CAN'T ADD

ART BUCHWALD

Mr. Buchwald is one of the more effective people presently trying to keep matters in perspective—that is, keep
his head when all around him, people are losing theirs.
In his regular columns in the newspapers, he pokes fun
at most everyone, from the President down to the low-
liest bureaucrat, and at most everything, including the
New Math. Perhaps you'll recognize some of the strange
business which confuses him in this little essay.

There has been a great deal of discussion about American
education in the last ten years and everyone has come up
with his theory as to why Johnny can't add. I know why
Johnny can't add. It's because his parents can't do his
homework.

In the old days before N.M. (New Math) a kid could
bring home his homework and his parents would go over it
with him, making corrections or suggestions, and giving encouragement when the going got rough. But today the parent is in the soup because the homework is so complicated
that neither the kid nor his parent knows what is going on.

For example, the other day my daughter brought home
a homework assignment.

"I have to subtract 179 from 202," she said.

"It's quite simple," I said, "you put the 202 over the 179."

"But what do I do with the 10?"

"What 10?"

"The 10 that goes next to the 202."

"I don't know what 10 goes next to the 202. Let's subtract 179 from 202. Nine from two is three, and you carry one. Eight from zero is two. The answer is 23."

"We can't do it that way. We have to use a 10."

"Why 10?"

"Ten is a unit."

"I see. Well, the answer is still 23," I said.

"How do you know?"

"Because I took nine from two and eight from zero."

"That's not the way to do it."

"Oh, yeah? Well, that's the way I did it."

"My teacher says you can't take nine from two."

"Why not?"

"Because you can't borrow from something you don't give back."

"Well, I'm going to call your teacher and see how she subtracts 179 from 202."

I placed a call to my daughter's teacher and explained I was having a small problem with the homework she had assigned.

The teacher was very nice on the phone. "It's really quite simple," she said. "The two in the right-hand column is considered units of one. The zero in the center counts for zero tens. The two in the left-hand column counts for hundreds. Therefore, you have two hundreds, zero tens, and two ones."

"You're putting me on," I said.

"Now to subtract," she said. "Go to the hundreds column and start regrouping. Two hundred will become 100. Therefore, bring this 10 to the tens column. Now you have 10 tens, but you still can't subtract in the units column. Therefore, regroup again. Now you only have nine tens. Take 12 from the 10 and now bring it over to the ones column because 10 ones equal one. Now you have 12 ones. Do you understand?"

"What's there not to understand?" I said. "Can I ask you a very, very personal question?"

"Yes, of course."

"Is the answer 23?"

"In this case it is, but it isn't necessarily 23. If you were working in units other than 10, it could be something else."

I hung up and started swallowing a whole bottle of aspirin, but my wife caught me in time. "How many aspirins did you take?" she asked.

"I took seven and then I took five, but don't ask me what it adds up to."

8

A MATHEMATICAL PROBLEM
SAMUEL TAYLOR COLERIDGE

Back a hundred years or so, when I was a school-boy myself, we studied, analyzed and committed portions to memory of the poem *The Ancient Mariner*, by Samuel Taylor Coleridge. From this poem come such lines as "Water, water everywhere and not a drop to drink;" (though really it is "nor any drop to drink;") and "Instead of the cross the albatross around my neck was hung."

As I understand it, *The Ancient Mariner* is no longer part of the curriculum, and you may have to take my word for the fact that Mr. Coleridge was quite a well-thought-of poet, who happened to turn his thoughts occasionally to mathematics. As you will see from the letter which introduced this poem, mathematics did not enjoy a particularly high reputation among the non-math people of the late eighteenth century.

Incidentally, or, maybe, not so incidentally, you will find a new annotated edition of *The Ancient Mariner* available now, with the annotation done by a mathematician, Martin Gardner.

MATHEMATICAL PROBLEM

If Pegasus will let thee only ride him,
Spurning my clumsy efforts to o'erstride him,
Some fresh expedient the Muse will try,
And walk on stilts, although she cannot fly.

To the Rev. George Coleridge

DEAR BROTHER,

I have often been surprised that Mathematics, the quintessence of Truth, should have found admirers so few and so languid. Frequent consideration and minute scrutiny have at length unravelled the cause; viz. that though Reason is feasted, Imagination is starved; whilst Reason is luxuriating in its proper Paradise, Imagination is wearily travelling on a dreary desert. To assist Reason by the stimulous of Imagination is the design of the following production. In the execution of it much may be objectionable. The verse (particularly in the introduction of the ode) may be accused of unwarrantable liberties, but they are liberties equally homogeneal with the exactness of Mathematical disquisition, and the boldness of Pindaric daring. I have three strong champions to defend me against the attacks of Criticism: the Novelty, the Difficulty, and the Utility of the work. I may just plume myself that I first have drawn the nymph Mathesis from the visionary caves of abstracted idea, and caused her to unite with Harmony. The first-born of this Union I now present to you; with interested motives indeed —as I expect to receive in return the more valuable offspring of your Muse.

Thine ever,

[CHRIST'S HOSPITAL], *March* 31, 1791.   S. T. C.

This is now—this was erst,
Proposition the first—and Problem the first.

I

On a given finite line
Which must no way incline;
To describe an equi—
—lateral Tri—
—A, N, G, L, E.   5
Now let A. B.
Be the given line
Which must no way incline;
The great Mathematician
Makes this Requisition,   10
That we describe an Equi—
—lateral Tri—
—angle on it:
Aid us, Reason—aid us, Wit!

II

From the centre A. at the distance A. B.   15
Describe the circle B. C. D.
At the distance B. A. from B. the centre
The round A. C. E. to describe boldly venture.
(Third postulate see.)
And from the point C.   20
In which the circles make a pother
Cutting and slashing one another,
Bid the straight lines a journeying go.
C. A. C. B. those lines will show.
To the points, which by A. B. are reckon'd,   25

37

And postulate the second
For Authority ye know.
A. B. C.
Triumphant shall be
An Equilateral Triangle,   30
Not Peter Pindar carp, nor Zoilus can wrangle.

III

Because the point A. is the centre
Of the circular B. C. D.
And because the point B. is the centre
Of the circular A. C. E.   35
A. C. to A. B. and B. C. to B. A.
Harmoniously equal for ever must stay;
Then C. A. and B. C.
Both extend the kind hand
To the basis, A. B.   40
Unambitiously join'd in Equality's Band.
But to the same powers, when two powers are equal,
My mind forbodes the sequel;
My mind does some celestial impulse teach,
And equalises each to each.   45
Thus C. A. with B. C. strikes the same sure alliance,
That C. A. and B. C. had with A. B. before;
And in mutual affiance
None attempting to soar
Above another,   50
The unanimous three
C. A. and B. C. and A. B.
All are equal, each to his brother.

9

A CIRCLE'S THOUGHTS

JAIME JUAN FALCON

Since the time of the Greeks, mathematicians and most everyone else has tried to solve this problem: With compass and straightedge, construct a square with its area the same as the area of a given circle. This was finally shown (in the nineteenth century) to be impossible. But much mathematics was produced along the way. In fact, even today, people continue to try to "square the circle."

To my knowledge, only one person has given much thought to how a circle feels about being reduced to a square. He was Jaime Juan Falcon, a sixteenth-century Spanish poet. Falcon was also an amateur mathematician, who published a book on the squaring of the circle.

Here is his poem, translated by Professor Lincoln G. Hendrickson.

I used to be called a circle
and I was curved on all sides
like the lofty orbit of the sun
and the arc of the rainbow in the clouds.
I was a noble figure
the only one without beginning
the only one without an end.

39

But recently I have emerged
in indecorous form
made foul by new angles.
This neither Archytis accomplished
nor the father of Icarus (Dedalus)
nor you, the son of Japhetus (Prometheus)
Therefore, what God has squared my area?
At the high gates of Turia
and its limpid lake there is a happy city.
Segunto is not far away
and Sucro only a little distant.

Here lives a certain poet
gladly consulting with the stars
claiming for himself things denied the more learned.
An old man, forever in thought
often forgetful of himself,
not knowing how to open the compasses
nor how to draw the straight lines
as he readily confesses.
Yet this artist has squared your area.

10

GETTING FROM JANUARY TO DECEMBER

WILL CUPPY

The titles of Will Cuppy's books
How to be a Hermit
How to Tell Your Friends from the Apes
How to Become Extinct
How to Attract the Wombat
The Decline and Fall of Practically Everybody
bely the fact that he was an extremely painstaking
researcher. And, 'tis not surprising that in his research
he should touch upon matters mathematical, both applied and biographical. Perhaps it is just as well that
"pure mathematics" did not fit into his writing plans,
for, as you will see from these selections, Mr. Cuppy did
not take anything terribly seriously, and, from what
I have been able to see, "pure mathematics" is a
very serious proposition.

Anyway, here are some selections from *How to Get
from January to December*, which was published after
Mr. Cuppy's death in 1949. Appropriately enough, I
think, he included some remarks on the business of
reforming the calendar, which has attracted the attention of such people as Julius Caesar, assorted popes,
Omar Khayyam, and even mathematicians. Getting
from January to December involves taking each day
as it comes. For instance, there must be a . . .

FEBRUARY 28

I don't seem to have heard whether anything has been done lately about reforming the calendar. The plan, you know, was to fix the calendar so that the same day would fall on the same date every year, if that's the way to put it. For instance June 6 would fall on Wednesday every year, instead of Thursday, as it did in 1935, or Tuesday, as in 1933, or Sunday, as in 1875. This can be done by giving March, May, August, and December only thirty days each, instead of thirty-one, taking one day from April, stabilizing February at thirty, having a thing called Year Day between December 30 and January 1, and another thing called Leap Day right after June 30 when necessary. It might be fun.

There will be trouble, I'll bet, from people whose birthdays occur on March 31, May 31, August 31 or December 31, because there won't be any such dates any more. Well, those born December 31 will just have to celebrate on Year Day and like it. Besides, my own birthday is August 23. All in all, I withdraw any objections I may have to calendar reform in the past. It really looks as though it might provide a rational method of telling what day it is without going down cellar and scrabbing through a lot of old newspapers—which generally leaves you about where you were, anyway.

Actually, adoption of the calendar reform that Mr. Cuppy advocated would be particularly unfortunate right now. For, it was only the other day that someone was telling me about a great way to use one or another facet of the *New Math*. Seems a chap showed how you could use NEW MATH to determine how many, say, Thursdays the thirteenth there are in a given year— or Tuesdays the twenty-fifth, and so on. If the calendar were changed the way Mr. Cuppy describes it, the problem would be solved in one try for all years, and then what would we do with the New Math?

Mr. Cuppy also dealt with this matter of weights and measures, which seems to have mathematical implications. At least, I used to find matters such as these discussed in mathematics books. In particular, the strange assortment sometimes called "the British system"—pounds, inches, acres, gills, hogsheads, etc.— have given many a struggling young math scholar fits. So, here we go with "April 11," which Mr. Cuppy introduces via a cheery letter from one of his readers.

"Dear Sir: What do the English mean by the expression, 'Cholmondeley weighs fourteen stone?'"

"Bothered"

They mean that Cholmondeley weighs fourteen times fourteen pounds, or 196 pounds—a stone equaling fourteen pounds avoirdupois in their language when applied to Englishmen or other large animals—otherwise, a stone equals anywhere from eight to twenty-four pounds. Apparently they do not wish to say right out that Cholmondeley weighs 196 pounds, and in my opinion they don't even know it. Since the human brain is not so constituted as to be able to multiply fourteens at will there is always a large margin of uncertainty about people's weights in England. They get some sort of general impression, however, and that seems to satisfy them.

Or, how about a little "compound interest?" There's a really fine application of mathematics. I'm not at all sure what this discussion has to do with May 18, unless it is that if you deposit money at compound interest on May 18, the bank will probably enter something in your bank book around May 18 of the next year.

You may want to mull that over *after* you have read Mr. Cuppy's remarks on this facet of applied mathematics.

MAY 18

If you saved a nickel every day for a year, at the end of that period you would have 365 nickels, or 366 in Leap Year. It sounds quite wonderful until you think it out. The catch is that you might have been spending the nickels all that time.

Supposing you are a strong character, however, and have succeeded in saving 365 nickels. You have $18.25. Your next move is to put it out at compound interest, as you would be quite capable of doing if you could save nickels in the first place.

You'd be amazed how compound interest counts up, especially when it's compounded every three months. At the end of their first year of work at 2½ per cent compound interest—that is, two years after you saved the first one—your nickels will have earned you the neat little sum of $0.46. (I really thought the figures would be more impressive, or I wouldn't have started this.)

The smartest plan is to begin saving your nickels when you're a child. I understand that a nickel at 4 per cent compound interest, if you can find somebody who'll give you 4 per cent, will just about double itself in forty-five years. Or better yet, have somebody deposit a whopping big sum that you can get at the minute you come of age.

You can find many people around these days who contend that mathematics is really just logic, or, that logic is really just mathematics. I think that, one way or another, this point of view slights mathematics no little and quite some, as Damon Runyon used to say. But, the association is with us, and I hear people going around saying to young math types and non-math types, "You should take a course in logic."

If you haven't encountered logic before, Mr. Cuppy's remarks which follow should be a good introduction. Syllogisms seem to play an important part in logic.

APRIL 17

In addition to other forms of nonsense, Aristotle is credited with promoting the syllogism, if not actually inventing it.

That's the line of reasoning that goes like this:

> Socrates is rational;
> Socrates is a man;
> Therefore, man is rational.

Even at the time, everybody knew perfectly well that Socrates was not rational. Subsequently an unsung Great Thinker has pointed out that "the major premise of the syllogism takes for granted precisely the point to be proved."

These days syllogisms have given way to Twenty Questions and Charades. All to the good, I'd say.

Of course, Mr. Cuppy was writing back in the 1940s. The current status might be expressed as follows: Logic is IN. Syllogisms are part of logic. Therefore, syllogisms are IN. Mr. Cuppy probably wouldn't like it.

The calendar must have been one of Mr. Cuppy's "things" for here it is again, on July 12. Of course, Omar Khayyam had the whole thing figured out in the eleventh century—and a better calendar than we use today. But, since Edward Fitzgerald who rediscovered Omar was more interested in Persian poetry, we still hear little about Omar's calendar, and have to live with the error of .0003 days that Mr. Cuppy mentions.

JULY 12

"Dear Sir: The next time Julius Caesar's birthday occurs, please tell me what he actually did about the calendar, instead of just stalling around in your usual way. Give us some definite facts and figures."

"Scholarly"

I have been saving your question until today, as Gaius Julius Caesar was born July 12, 102 B.C. He didn't do as much about the calendar as you might imagine. The real credit should go to Sosigenes of Alexandria, a Greek astronomer and mathematician, who was called in for the brainwork, or what passed for brainwork in those days.

46

Sosigenes had achieved fame by writing a treatise on revolving spheres—without, it must be confessed, knowing a
great deal about revolving spheres. Anyway, Caesar grabbed
him to ghost his calendar.

Sosigenes was faced by the problem of finding the exact
number of days in what is called the tropical year, which
is roughly the interval of time between two dates when the
sun in its apparent motion around the eliptic circle (an
imaginary line), attains its greatest angular distance from
the celestial equator (another imaginary line)—you asked
for it, *Scholarly*. Now this interval contains 365.2422 days,
or 365 days, 5 hours, 48 minutes and 48 seconds. You
would hardly expect Sosigenes to figure *that* out, and you
would be right. He didn't, and the whole thing had to be
done over again.

p.s. There is still an error of .0003 days per year in our
calendar. My advice is to forget about it.

47

11

AN EXPLANATION OF THE FACT THAT THERE HAVE BEEN VERY FEW . . . IN FACT . . . VERY, VERY FEW LADY MATHEMATICIANS THROUGHOUT THE HISTORY OF MATHEMATICS

CHARLES F. LINN

You may have heard it said that mathematics is a man's game . . . that for some reason or another, the ladies just can't handle this esoteric stuff. Try to find out why, though, and you usually receive unsatisfactory answers—vague remarks—suggestions that this is a stupid question, and so on.

But, as you know, much that we do today is based upon traditions of one kind or another that have their roots in that "dim antiquity" that people talk about. I have suspected (since many of my best math students have been gals) that this business of ladies and mathematics may go back to that same "dim antiquity." The recent discovery of fragments of the diary of a young lady in ancient Greece has brought evidence which supports my theory.

Here, then, is an excerpt from the diary of Zoe, daughter of Ariston of Athens . . .

Today I had a fun time over at old Plato's. I suppose I should be more respectful, but he is such a fuddy-duddy. Daddy decided that I should study mathematics, and this seemed like a good idea to me, since I got interested in what he and his friends were saying the other evening about how the Egyptians built their pyramids and things like that.

So, since Daddy's got half the money in this town, he wrangled a deal with Plato for me to take lessons in mathematics. Today was my first, and, I'm afraid, my last lesson. Daddy's going to be upset when he hears, and I guess I am impertinent, but Plato's such a square. Poor Daddy, it's too bad he didn't have half a dozen boys, or at least one, instead of me.

Anyway, I went over to Plato's at the appointed hour. One of his slaves led me to the little garden where the old boy was sitting, half asleep it looked like to me, but the slave said he was thinking. I went up to him as cheerfully as possible and said, "Hi, Plato."

He sat up, scowled, and said, "I suppose you are Ariston's daughter," and, "You will call me 'Professor,' if you please."

Well, I didn't please, since everyone else seems to call him just "Plato." But I guessed I would humor him, so I agreed and sat on a low wall near the old boy, kicked off my sandals, and prepared to learn some mathematics.

Plato looked at me with obvious displeasure. "I am accustomed," he said, "to have my pupils sit at my feet."

I told him I didn't want to sit on the ground with all the bugs and I could hear just as well from where I was. He didn't seem very happy about this, and, after frowning quietly for a minute, said, "I have never attempted to instruct a female pupil before." The way he looked at me indicated that he had decided already that this was a waste of time.

But he began. "First I will tell you about the tools of the geometer, since geometry is the only mathematics worth considering." He called for a servant to bring out a couple of gadgets he called compasses, and a piece of iron with a straight edge. "With this equipment," he intoned, "you can perform all the geometric constructions."

"What about the Delian Problem?" I asked, for that had fascinated me when Daddy and his friends talked about it.

"Silence, girl," the old boy scowled. (He's a great scowler.) "You are here to learn." Then he went on with the speech. "Now to bisect an angle, you first make marks with the compasses."

"But, Plato," I said, in my excitement forgetting all about calling him Professor, "why not just measure the angle with that little gadget the Egyptians used? Talos thinks they got the idea from the Sumerians many years ago."

"Silence!"—and this time he really roared. "What do those Egyptians know about geometry? They are technicians. They play with blocks . . . they . . . they . . ." And the way he sputtered and shook I thought he was going to have a heart attack. I sure shut up, and after a while he simmered down, and began again.

"Now, where was I? Yes, you then take this straightedge and place it across the points you marked with your compasses . . ."

But I had a great idea. "Look," I said, "why don't you make some marks on that piece of iron. You could mark it off evenly, and then measure with it like the Egyptians did with their knots in the rope . . ."

Gee, the old boy really blew his stack on that one. The slaves came running, and I decided I'd better eclipse myself, as the ancient Sumerians used to say. I grabbed my sandals and ran out.

Guess that's the end of my mathematics lessons. But, if

you've got to do things in such stupid, inefficient ways, I don't think I want to study mathematics anyway.

I guess I'll have to tell Daddy, and then he's going to be mad.

Now, I'm not saying for sure that this started the whole business about women not being good at math. But Plato's ideas have carried a lot of weight, even down to the present . . . and, it's just possible . . .

12

EUCLID

VACHEL LINDSAY

Old Euclid drew a circle
On a sand-beach long ago.
He bound it and enclosed it
With angles thus and so.
His set of solemn graybeards
Nodded and argued much,
Of arc and circumference
Diameter and Such.
A silent child stood by them
From morning until noon,
Because they drew such charming
Round pictures of the moon.

MATHEMATICIANS
IN
STRANGE PLACES

13

THE FEELING OF POWER

ISAAC ASIMOV

If you've read any science fiction, you'll recognize the name of Isaac Asimov, and this brief introduction will be redundant. If you haven't read any science fiction, you can do no better than begin with an Asimov story. This one happens to be a particular favorite of mine, and I hope you like it.

Dr. Asimov, who is a biochemist by trade, has written an amazing number of excellent books on science and mathematics, as well as some really first-rate science fiction. After teaching for a number of years at Boston University, he dropped out of the academic scene and has been concentrating on his writing.

I include his story in this section, since he certainly could not be classified as a "stranger in mathematical places." Though not a mathematician, in that he does not make his living at doing mathematics, he comes close enough for my practical purpose of classification here.

Jehan Shuman was used to dealing with the men in authority on long-embattled earth. He was only a civilian but he originated programming patterns that resulted in self-directing war computers of the highest sort. Generals consequently listened to him. Heads of congressional committees too.

There was one of each in the special lounge of New Pentagon. General Weider was space-burned and had a small mouth puckered almost into a cipher. Congressman Brant was smooth-cheeked and clear-eyed. He smoked Denebian tobacco with the air of one whose patriotism was so notorious, he could be allowed such liberties.

Shuman, tall, distinguished, and Programmer-first-class, faced them fearlessly.

He said, "This, gentlemen, is Myron Aub."

"The one with the unusual gift that you discovered quite by accident," said Congressman Brant placidly. "Ah." He inspected the little man with the egg-bald head with amiable curiosity.

The little man, in return, twisted the fingers of his hands anxiously. He had never been near such great men before. He was only an aging low-grade technician who had long ago failed all tests designed to smoke out the gifted ones among mankind and had settled into the rut of unskilled labor. There was just this hobby of his that the great Programmer had found out about and was now making such a frightening fuss over.

General Weider said, "I find this atmosphere of mystery childish."

"You won't in a moment," said Shuman. "This is not something we can leak to the firstcomer. Aub!" There was something imperative about his manner of biting off that one-syllable name, but then he was a great Programmer speaking to a mere technician. "Aub! How much is nine times seven?"

Aub hesitated a moment. His pale eyes glimmered with a feeble anxiety. "Sixty-three," he said.

Congressman Brant lifted his eyebrows. "Is that right?"

"Check it for yourself, Congressman."

The congressman took out his pocket computer, nudged the milled edges twice, looked at its face as it lay there in the palm of his hand, and put it back. He said, "Is this the gift you brought us here to demonstrate. An illusionist?"

"More than that, sir. Aub has memorized a few operations and with them he computes on paper."

"A paper computer?" said the general. He looked pained.

"No, sir," said Shuman patiently. "Not a paper computer. Simply a sheet of paper. General, would you be so kind as to suggest a number?"

"Seventeen," said the general.

"And you, Congressman?"

"Twenty-three."

"Good! Aub, multiply those numbers, and please show the gentlemen your manner of doing it."

"Yes, Programmer," said Aub, ducking his head. He fished a small pad out of one shirt pocket and an artist's hairline stylus out of the other. His forehead corrugated as he made painstaking marks on the paper.

General Weider interrupted him sharply. "Let's see that."

Aub passed him the paper, and Weider said, "Well, it looks like the figure seventeen."

Congressman Brant nodded and said, "So it does, but I suppose anyone can copy figures off a computer. I think I could make a passable seventeen myself, even without practice."

"If you will let Aub continue, gentlemen," said Shuman without heat.

Aub continued, his hand trembling a little. Finally he said

57

in a low voice, "The answer is three hundred and ninety-one."

Congressman Brant took out his computer a second time and flicked it. "By Godfrey, so it is. How did he guess?"

"No guess, Congressman," said Shuman. "He computed that result. He did it on this sheet of paper."

"Humbug," said the general impatiently. "A computer is one thing and marks on paper are another."

"Explain, Aub," said Shuman.

"Yes, Programmer. Well, gentlemen, I write down seventeen, and just underneath it I write twenty-three. Next I say to myself: seven times three—"

The congressman interrupted smoothly, "Now, Aub, the problem is seventeen times twenty-three."

"Yes, I know," said the little technician earnestly, "but I *start* by saying seven times three because that's the way it works. Now seven times three is twenty-one."

"And how do you know that?" asked the congressman.

"I just remember it. It's always twenty-one on the computer. I've checked it any number of times."

"That doesn't mean it always will be, though, does it?" said the congressman.

"Maybe not," stammered Aub. "I'm not a mathematician. But I always get the right answers, you see."

"Go on."

"Seven times three is twenty-one, so I write down twenty-one. Then one times three is three, so I write down a three under the two of twenty-one."

"Why under the two?" asked Congressman Brant at once.

"Because—" Aub looked helplessly at his superior for support. "It's difficult to explain."

58

Shuman said, "If you will accept his work for the moment, we can leave the details for the mathematicians."

Brant subsided.

Aub said, "Three plus two makes five, you see, so the twenty-one becomes a fifty-one. Now you let that go for a while and start fresh. You multiply seven and two, that's fourteen, and one and two, that's two. Put them down like this and it adds up to thirty-four. Now if you put the thirty-four under the fifty-one this way and add them, you get three hundred and ninety-one, and that's the answer."

There was an instant's silence and then General Weider said, "I don't believe it. He goes through this rigmarole and makes up numbers and multiplies and adds them this way and that, but I don't believe it. It's too complicated to be anything but horn-swoggling."

"Oh no, sir," said Aub in a sweat. "It only *seems* complicated because you're not used to it. Actually the rules are quite simple and will work for any numbers."

"Any numbers, eh?" said the general. "Come, then." He took out his own computer (a severely styled GI model) and struck it at random. "Make a five seven three eight on the paper. That's five thousand seven hundred and thirty-eight."

"Yes, sir," said Aub, taking a new sheet of paper.

"Now"—more punching of his computer—"seven two three nine. Seven thousand two hundred and thirty-nine."

"Yes, sir."

"And now multiply those two."

"It will take some time," quavered Aub.

"Take the time," said the general.

"Go ahead, Aub," said Shuman crisply.

Aub set to work, bending low. He took another sheet of

paper and another. The general took out his watch finally and stared at it. "Are you through with your magic-making, Technician?"

"I'm almost done, sir. Here it is, sir. Forty-one million, five hundred and thirty-seven thousand, three hundred and eighty-two." He showed the scrawled figures of the result.

General Weider smiled bitterly. He pushed the multiplication contact on his computer and let the numbers whirl to a halt. And then he stared and said in a surprised squeak, "Great Galaxy, the fella's right."

The President of the Terrestrial Federation had grown haggard in office and, in private, he allowed a look of settled melancholy to appear on his sensitive features. The Denebian War, after its early start of vast movement and great popularity, had trickled down into a sordid matter of maneuver and counter-maneuver, with discontent rising steadily on earth. Possibly, it was rising on Deneb too.

And now Congressman Brant, head of the important Committee on Military Appropriations, was cheerfully and smoothly spending his half-hour appointment spouting nonsense.

"Computing without a computer," said the president impatiently, "is a contradiction in terms."

"Computing," said the congressman, "is only a system for handling data. A machine might do it, or the human brain might. Let me give you an example." And, using the new skills he had learned, he worked out sums and products until the president, despite himself, grew interested.

"Does this always work?"

"Every time, Mr. President. It is foolproof."

"Is it hard to learn?"

"It took me a week to get the real hang of it. I think you would do better."

"Well," said the president, considering, "it's an interesting parlor game, but what is the use of it?"

"What is the use of a newborn baby, Mr. President? At the moment there is no use, but don't you see that this points the way toward liberation from the machine. Consider, Mr. President"—the congressman rose and his deep voice automatically took on some of the cadences he used in public debate—"that the Denebian War is a war of computer against computer. Their computers forge an impenetrable shield of countermissiles against our missiles, and ours forge one against theirs. If we advance the efficiency of our computers, so do they theirs, and for five years a precarious and profitless balance has existed.

"Now we have in our hands a method for going beyond the computed, leapfrogging it, passing through it. We will combine the mechanics of computation with human thought; we will have the equivalent of intelligent computers, billions of them. I can't predict what the consequences will be in detail, but they will be incalculable. And if Deneb beats us to the punch, they may be unimaginably catastrophic."

The president said, troubled, "What would you have me do?"

"Put the power of the administration behind the establishment of a secret project on human computation. Call it Project Number, if you like. I can vouch for my committee, but I will need the administration behind me."

"But how far can human computation go?"

"There is no limit. According to Programmer Shuman, who first introduced me to this discovery—"

"I've heard of Shuman, of course."

"Yes. Well, Dr. Shuman tells me that in theory there is nothing the computer can do that the human mind cannot do. The computer merely takes a finite amount of data and performs a finite number of operations upon them. The human mind can duplicate the process."

The president considered that. He said, "If Shuman says this, I am inclined to believe him—in theory. But, in practice, how can anyone know how a computer works?"

Brant laughed genially. "Well, Mr. President, I asked the same question. It seems that at one time computers were designed directly by human beings. Those were simple computers, of course, this being before the time of the rational use of computers to design more advanced computers had been established."

"Yes, yes. Go on."

"Technician Aub apparently had, as his hobby, the reconstruction of some of these ancient devices, and in so doing he studied the details of their workings and found he could imitate them. The multiplication I just performed for you is an imitation of the workings of a computer."

"Amazing!"

The congressman coughed gently. "If I may make another point, Mr. President—the further we can develop this thing, the more we can divert our federal effort from computer production and computer maintenance. As the human brain takes over, more of our energy can be directed into peacetime pursuits and the impingement of war on the ordinary man will be less. This will be most advantageous for the party in power, of course."

"Ah," said the president, "I see your point. Well, sit down, Congressman, sit down. I want some time to think about this. But meanwhile, show me that multiplication trick again. Let's see if I can't catch the point of it."

Programmer Shuman did not try to hurry matters. Loesser was conservative, very conservative, and liked to deal with computers as his father and grandfather had. Still, he controlled the West European computer combine, and if he could be persuaded to join Project Number in full enthusiasm, a great deal would be accomplished.

But Loesser was holding back. He said, "I'm not sure I like the idea of relaxing our hold on computers. The human mind is a capricious thing. The computer will give the same answer to the same problem each time. What guarantee have we that the human mind will do the same?"

"The human mind, Computer Loesser, only manipulates facts. It doesn't matter whether the human mind or a machine does it. They are just tools."

"Yes, yes. I've gone over your ingenious demonstration that the mind can duplicate the computer, but it seems to me a little in the air. I'll grant the theory, but what reason have we for thinking that theory can be converted to practice?"

"I think we have reason, sir. After all, computers have not always existed. The cave men with their triremes, stone axes, and railroads had no computers."

"And possibly they did not compute."

"You know better than that. Even the building of a railroad or ziggurat called for some computing, and that must have been without computers as we know them."

"Do you suggest they computed in the fashion you demonstrate?"

"Probably not. After all, this method—we call it 'graphit-

63

ics,' by the way, from the old European word 'grapho,' meaning 'to write'—is developed from the computers themselves, so it cannot have antedated them. Still, the cave men must have had *some* method, eh?"

"Lost arts! If you're going to talk about lost arts—"

"No, no. I'm not a lost art enthusiast, though I don't say there may not be some. After all, man was eating grain before hydroponics, and if the primitives ate grain, they must have grown it in soil. What else could they have done?"

"I don't know, but I'll believe in soil growing when I see someone grow grain in soil. And I'll believe in making fire by rubbing two pieces of flint together when I see that too."

Shuman grew placative. "Well, let's stick to graphitics. It's just part of the process of etherealization. Transportation by means of bulky contrivances is giving way to direct mass transference. Communications devices become less massive and more efficient constantly. For that matter, compare your pocket computer with the massive jobs of a thousand years ago. Why not, then, the last step of doing away with computers altogether? Come, sir, Project Number is a going concern; progress is already headlong. But we want your help. If patriotism doesn't move you, consider the intellectual adventure involved."

Loesser said skeptically, "What progress? What can you do beyond multiplication? Can you integrate a transcendental function?"

"In time, sir. In time. In the last month I have learned to handle division. I can determine, and correctly, integral quotients and decimal quotients."

"Decimal quotients? To how many places?"

Programmer Shuman tried to keep his tone casual. "Any number!"

Loesser's lower jaw dropped. "Without a computer?"

"Set me a problem."

"Divide twenty-seven by thirteen. Take it to six places."

Five minutes later Shuman said, "Two point oh seven six nine two three."

Loesser checked it. "Well, now, that's amazing. Multiplication didn't impress me too much because it involved integers, after all, and I thought trick manipulation might do it. But decimals—"

"And that is not all. There is a new development that is, so far, top secret and which, strictly speaking, I ought not to mention. Still—we may have made a break-through on the square root front."

"Square roots?"

"It involves some tricky points and we haven't licked the bugs yet, but Technician Aub, the man who invented the science and who has an amazing intuition in connection with it, maintains he has the problem almost solved. And he is only a technician. A man like yourself, a trained and talented mathematician, ought to have no difficulty."

"Square roots," muttered Loesser, attracted.

"Cube roots, too. Are you with us?"

Loesser's hand thrust out suddenly. "Count me in."

General Weider stumped his way back and forth at the head of the room and addressed his listeners after the fashion of a savage teacher facing a group of recalcitrant students. It made no difference to the general that they were the civilian scientists heading Project Number. The general was the over-all head, and he so considered himself at every waking moment.

He said, "Now square roots are all fine. I can't do them

65

myself and I don't understand the methods, but they're fine. Still, the project will not be sidetracked into what some of you call the fundamentals. You can play with graphitics any way you want to after the war is over, but right now we have specific and very practical problems to solve."

In a far corner Technician Aub listened with painful attention. He was no longer a technician, of course, having been relieved of his duties and assigned to the project, with a fine-sounding title and good pay. But, of course, the social distinction remained, and the highly placed scientific leaders could never bring themselves to admit him to their ranks on a footing of equality. Nor, to do Aub justice, did he, himself, wish it. He was as uncomfortable with them as they with him.

The general was saying, "Our goal is a simple one, gentlemen—the replacement of the computer. A ship that can navigate space without a computer on board can be constructed in one fifth the time and at one tenth the expense of a computer-laden ship. We could build fleets five times, ten times, as great as Deneb could if we could but eliminate the computer.

"And I see something even beyond this. It may be fantastic now, a mere dream, but in the future I see the manned missile!"

There was an instant murmur from the audience.

The general drove on. "At the present time our chief bottleneck is the fact that missiles are limited in intelligence. The computer controlling them can only be so large, and for that reason they can meet the changing nature of anti-missile defenses in an unsatisfactory way. Few missiles, if any, accomplish their goal, and missile warfare is coming to a dead end, for the enemy, fortunately, as well as for ourselves.

"On the other hand, a missile with a man or two within, controlling flight by graphitics, would be lighter, more mobile, more intelligent. It would give us a lead that might well mean the margin of victory. Besides which, gentlemen, the exigencies of war compel us to remember one thing. A man is much more dispensable than a computer. Manned missiles could be launched in numbers and under circumstances that no good general would care to undertake as far as computer-directed missiles are concerned . . ."

He said much more, but Technician Aub did not wait.

Technician Aub, in the privacy of his quarters, labored long over the note he was leaving behind. It read finally as follows:

"When I began the study of what is now called graphitics, it was no more than a hobby. I saw no more in it than an interesting amusement, an exercise of mind.

"When Project Number began, I thought that others were wiser than I, that graphitics might be put to practical use as a benefit to mankind, to aid in the production of really practical mass-transference devices perhaps. But now I see it is to be used only for death and destruction.

"I cannot face the responsibility involved in having invented graphitics."

He then deliberately turned the focus of a protein depolarizer on himself and fell instantly and painlessly dead.

They stood over the grave of the little technician while tribute was paid to the greatness of his discovery.

Programmer Shuman bowed his head along with the rest

of them but remained unmoved. The technician had done his share and was no longer needed, after all. He might have started graphitics, but now that it had started, it would carry on by itself overwhelmingly, triumphantly, until manned missiles were possible with who knew what else.

Nine times seven, thought Shuman with deep satisfaction, is sixty-three, and I don't need a computer to tell me so. The computer is in my head.

And it was amazing the feeling of power that it gave him.

14

THE WISE MAN OF SUMATRA
DAVID EUGENE SMITH

David Eugene Smith was one of the great American mathematics teachers, and probably the greatest math historian. He also wrote many children's stories involving mathematics, and an occasional story that did not involve mathematics at all. I think it appropriate that he should be represented in this volume by one of those non-mathematical writings. Professor Smith wrote this story, while he was in India, for a young friend in a hospital back in the United States.

There is a place on the side of a mountain in Sumatra where three trees snug up together. One is a rubber tree, one is a banana tree, and one is a date palm. On a straw mat in the shade of these trees sits, cross-legged, a man with long black hair and long whiskers. This is the Wise Man of Sumatra. About a hundred feet to his right is a stone post with a straight mark across the top. About a hundred feet to his left is a spring of water. Beside the mat are a water jug, two cups, and a copper pan. The Wise Man sits with his eyes closed; he is thinking. He says to himself, "It is ten o'clock in the morning here; I am just on the other side of the earth from New York; it is ten o'clock at night there; I will motion to Russell Wood to come."

Two minutes later the Wise Man looked way off over the valley, way off over the sea, way off to the west, and there he saw a speck in the sky. It grew larger and larger, it came nearer and nearer, it sailed right down near the Wise Man's mat, and Russell Wood stepped up and said, "How do you do, Mr. Wise Man?"

Then the Wise Man asked Russell to sit down and tell him what he wanted to see. "I learned in my geography," said he, "that the equator runs east and west through Sumatra, and I would like to see that."

"But how can anything run east and west?" asked the Wise Man. "It would either run plump into itself, or else it would break in two, one part running east and the other part west. Beside, how can the equator run anyway; it hasn't any legs?"

"I don't know," said Russell, "all I know about it is what the geography says."

"That is just like a geography. Now the equator is only a hundred feet from you, and you don't see it run. I don't believe you see it at all. There is a mark on top of that post that tells where the equator is. You may go see it if you wish."

"But my geography says that it's hot on the equator. Will it burn me?"

"Well, I boil my water for my tea on the equator," said the Wise Man. "I will show you how." Then he stretched his arm out three feet and took the water jug; then he stretched it out a hundred feet and filled the jug at the spring; then he shortened his arm and poured the water into the pan; then he stretched it out again and put it on the ground just over the equator, and in two minutes the water was boiling. Then he shortened his arm, put the pan of water beside the mat, took some tea leaves from his pocket, made some tea, and asked Russell if he would drink some with him. But Russell was too astonished to think of tea.

"How did you stretch your arm like that?" he asked.

"Oh, it is easy enough. Don't you stretch in bed when you wake up?"

"Yes, but I don't stretch my arm a hundred feet. I couldn't do it. How do you make your hand go way out like that?"

"It's just because I drink rubber milk," said the Wise Man.

"This is the first time I ever heard of rubber milk. Do you have rubber cows in Sumatra?"

"No, I get it from this rubber tree," and taking his knife he cut the bark and some milk came out. "It is of this milk that rubber is made. If I drink rubber milk, I can stretch as far as I wish." Saying this, the Wise Man stretched his neck up where the dates were growing on the palm tree, saw a nice bunch, and reached his hand up and picked it. Then he drew back and gave it to Russell. "You see, if you drank rubber milk as I do, you could stretch out your legs and walk over the trees," saying which his legs became eighty feet long and he walked a mile, over the trees and came back in three minutes.

Never had Russell seen or heard of anyone who could stretch like this. He could hardly believe it until the Wise Man took him in his arms and stretched up more than a thousand feet in the air—higher than any skyscraper in New York.

After they had their tea, the Wise Man said, "You know that the equator extends all the way around the earth. It goes around the place where we sit. We are inside the circle.

71

Now you walk over past that stone post and you will be south of the equator, but be careful not to step on it and get burned."

So Russell walked down by the post, jumped over the equator, and the Wise Man stretched out his arm and patted Russell on the head, saying, "Now you are again in a part of the world that the equator goes round, so you must be inside the circle. But you are outside the circle that you were in when you were here with me, aren't you?"

"Yes," said Russell.

"Then when you are outside the circle of the equator, you are inside it, aren't you?"

"Yes," said Russell, "but how can I be inside when I am outside, and outside when I'm inside?"

"It's always that way," said the Wise Man. "If you start at the west wall of your hospital and go east to the opposite wall, you are inside the building, aren't you? Well, if you go out doors and start at the west wall and keep going right around the earth you will come to the east wall, won't you? Well then you do just what you did before, so that you are inside the building."

"You are an awfully funny Wise Man," said Russell. "You make me say that the outside of a house is the inside and the inside is the outside."

"Certainly," said the Wise Man. "The inside of everything is the outside. You never can get out of a house, because you are always in it; and you can never get in it because you are always outside it. It is just as clear as that white is black."

"But it isn't," said Russell firmly. "White is always white and black is always black."

"Suppose," said the Wise Man, "that you look at a piece

72

of white paper in a perfectly dark room. What color do you see it to be?"

"Why it looks black."

"Exactly so, and now you see that white may be black and black may be white. It is all just as easy as to see that up is down."

"But it can't be," said Russell. "Up is up, and down is down, always."

"Now look at this picture," said the Wise Man. "In New York 'up' is towards the top of the paper. 'Down' is towards the bottom. But in Sumatra that same line seems to us up because it goes away from the center of the earth. So you see that 'up' and 'down' are both in the same direction."

He then ran his finger across the pencil lines of his drawing and rubbed them out. He could do this because he was mostly rubber, having lived on rubber milk. "Now," he said, "look at this circle of the earth. In New York you look to the east to see the sun rise; in Sumatra you look to the west to see it set. It is the same sun in the same position. So the right-hand part of the picture is east in New York and west in Sumatra. Therefore, east is the same as west, and west is the same as east. In the same way, north is south and south is north."

"Well is anything what it is?" asked Russell, "or is it what it isn't? I'm all mixed up."

"You will feel better after eating," said the Wise Man. "I will hold you up and you can pick a banana." So he took Russell in his arms and stretched out until the banana could be picked. "Now there is something about this banana tree that is curious. It grows so near the rubber tree that it drinks in lots of rubber milk. You take hold of one end of the banana and I will pull it out ten feet. There, you see

73

the banana is now ten feet long. I want only a couple of feet of it, and you may eat the rest."

Then the Wise Man looked at the sun and saw that it was about five o'clock in the afternoon in Sumatra, which is five in the morning in New York, so he said, "Your nurse will be looking for you in the hospital soon, so you had better put on the Wings of Thought and fly home."

"But what are the Wings of Thought?" asked Russell.

"They are what brought you here. A man can walk three miles an hour; a horse will go six miles an hour; a train, forty miles; an airplane one hundred miles; light will go 186,000 miles a second; but the Wings of Thought will go millions of miles in no time. You think of a certain star; it takes light four years to go that distance, but your thought goes there at once. So put on your Wings of Thought and think yourself back in Mineola."

"But it all seems to me like a dream."

"No, it is the real thing. You are here and I am here, and I am a Wise Rubber Man. What you in Mineola think is real is all a dream; what you think is a dream in Sumatra is all reality. When you wish you were not in the hospital just put on the Wings of Thought and come to me where all is real. Forget your hospital dream; come where the Wise Man can give you rubber milk, and where you can stretch a mile high. So good-bye for now, and dream you are back in Mineola where only three people are really real—yourself, your nurse, and Mrs. Weed. All the rest is a dream."

15

A MATH BOOK FOR THE QUEEN

CHARLES F. LINN

One bright day in the late 1860's, Queen Victoria of England received in the post a copy of *The Elements of Determinants* (*and their applications to Simultaneous Linear Equations and Algebraic Geometry*). The queen was astonished, to say the least, for mathematics was certainly not her strong point and she didn't even recognize the author, one Reverend Charles Lutwidge Dodgson, of Oxford University.

But, as a matter of fact, the queen had written to this gentleman after reading and being delighted with his earlier book, and had asked that she be sent a copy of his next book.

The earlier book, however, was *Alice in Wonderland,* which was more appealing to the queen, and that had been written under the pseudonym "Lewis Carroll." I suspect that you may not have heard of *The Elements of Determinants,* but the story of Alice has been a general favorite for over one hundred years.

Dodgson, they say, was not really much of a mathematician, though I can't refrain from observing that he was good enough to teach for many years at one of the leading universities of England. Perhaps his writing of children's fantasies was thought to put a knock on the academic community of his time, in the same way that some professors of our time are frowned upon for writing (and selling) science fiction stories.

I suspect, too, that the Reverend Dodgson may have been frowned upon by his clerical colleagues, for upon occasion he poked fun at ideas that were near and dear to their hearts. For example, the English theologian Isaac Watts once wrote a book called *Divine Songs for Children* which included the following poem entitled, of all things, "Against Idleness and Mischief."

> How does the little busy bee
>   Improve each shining hour,
> And gather honey all the day
>   From every opening flower.
>
> How skillfully she builds her cell!
>   How neat she spreads the wax!
> And labors hard to store it well
>   With the sweet food she makes.
>
> In works of labor or of skill
>   I would be busy too;
> For Satan finds some mischief still
>   For idle hands to do.
>
> In books, or work, or healthful play,
>   Let my first years be passed.
> That I may give for every day
>   Some good account at last.

Personally, I prefer Lewis Carroll's version—much less moralizing.

> How doth the little crocodile
>   Improve his shining tail,

76

And pour the waters of the Nile
On every golden scale.

How cheerfully he seems to grin
How neatly spreads his claws,
And welcomes little fishes in,
With gently smiling jaws!

Hooray for the mathematician's point of view.

16

CHAINS, LINKS AND DOUBLETS
LEWIS CARROLL

On 29 March 1879 the magazine *Vanity Fair* published a letter from "Lewis Carroll." The message said, in part:

Just a year ago last Christmas, two young ladies—smarting under that sorest scourge of feminine humanity, the having "nothing to do"—besought me to send them "some riddles." But riddles I had none of at hand, and therefore set myself to devise some other form of verbal torture which should serve the same purpose. The result of my meditations was a new kind of Puzzle—new at least to me—which now that it has been fairly tested by a year's experience, and commended by many friends, I offer to you, as a newly gathered nut . . .

The rules of the Puzzle are simple enough. Two words are proposed, of the same length; and the Puzzle consists in linking these together by interposing other words, each of which shall differ from the next word *in one letter only.* . . . The letters must not be interchanged among themselves, but each must keep to its own place . . . I call the two given words "a Doublet," the interposed words "Links," and the entire series "a Chain," of which I here append an example—

H E A D

H E A L

T E A L

T E L L

T A L L

T A I L

17

SYLLOGISMS
LEWIS CARROLL

Mathematicians, philosophers and other similarly disposed, are very fond of syllogisms, which are sequences of logical statements moving from premise to conclusion—all very seriously done, of course. Here is a nice serious mathematical example:

> All four-sided figures with four right angles
> are rectangles.
> A square has four right angles.
> Therefore, a square is a rectangle.

But Lewis Carroll proposed some less serious types of syllogisms:

> No kitten that loves fish is unteachable;
> No kitten without a tail will play with a gorilla;
> Kittens with whiskers always love fish;
> No teachable kitten has green eyes;
> No kittens have tails unless they have whiskers.

What conclusion do you draw from this? Why,

> No kitten with green eyes will play with a gorilla.
> Of course.

Prefer dogs? Here's another Lewis Carroll bit of logic:

No terriers wander among the signs of the zodiac;
Nothing, that does not wander
   among the signs of the zodiac, is a comet;
Nothing but a terrier has a curly tail.

Care to guess the next line? How about,
   No comet has a curly tail.

18

CARL FRIEDRICH
RUINS THE SCHOOLMASTER'S NAP

ROBERT A. ROSENBAUM

This is a true story about the young Carl Friedrich Gauss, who became one of the greatest mathematicians in history. It was written as the introduction to a booklet on arithmetic progressions which was never published, unfortunately. The author, Professor Rosenbaum, is one of those rare individuals who is both a mathematician and truly great teacher. He was chairman of the mathematics department at Wesleyan University in Middletown, Connecticut, but has forsaken the classroom to become the university vice-president for academic affairs and acting president. For several years Professor Rosenbaum was editor of the *American Mathematical Monthly,* the official publication of the Mathematical Association.

In the big schoolroom in Braunschweig, Germany, everyone was sleepy on this warm sunny afternoon. It was early summer of 1785, and the children were looking forward eagerly to vacation. During the lunch hour they had eaten as fast as they could, and then had run out to play games. By the time the school bell had rung for the start of the afternoon session, they were pretty tired; and, after they had settled down at their seats, they soon became drowsy.

82

But the sleepiest of all was Herr Buttner, the school-teacher. In this one-room school, he had to preside over about one hundred pupils, ranging in age from seven to fourteen, and they were more than a handful. A good many of the pupils were merely marking time until their confirmation date, when they would happily quit school and go to work. Herr Buttner had one powerful aid in keeping order and instilling learning—a big switch, which he used freely on the backs of his pupils to punish mischief or ignorance. The teacher had had a busy morning: hearing lessons in turn, walking up and down the aisles to ensure diligent attention to work, and exercising his strong right arm from time to time to restore wavering interests in study. Herr Buttner now regretted the heavy lunch he had eaten; as the afternoon session began, he sat behind his desk with his head in his hands, wishing with all his heart that he might take a little nap.

Unfortunately, he was faced with one of his hardest jobs: teaching arithmetic. Each child began the study of arithmetic at the age of nine, and continued with it until Herr Buttner thought he had mastered the subject, a state of affairs which almost never was reached before the pupil attained the age of fourteen and escaped from Herr Buttner's clutches. Thus, most of the students were in the arithmetic class. Moreover, they were at all stages of advancement. If only there were some way to give them all something to do, without the teacher's having to expend much energy! Herr Buttner rubbed his hands over his face —and had an inspiration.

"Ah," he thought to himself. "This'll keep 'em busy for a while."

Then he cleared his throat. "Boys!" he bellowed. "Get

out your slates." The children groaned. They didn't enjoy Herr Buttner's problems under the best of circumstances, and, on this warm afternoon, they would much have preferred hearing a story, or reading a book, as the pre-arithmetic group was to do—anything would have seemed better than the arithmetic problem which they knew was coming.

"All right, boys: here's what you do," ordered Herr Buttner. "Add up all the whole numbers from one to two hundred."

There was an immediate reaction from the class, subdued out of respect for the schoolmaster's switch. Under their voices the pupils whispered angrily: "All the numbers from one to two hundred?" "That's unfair!" "What a job!" "That'll take all afternoon!"

Herr Buttner smiled with satisfaction. He foresaw a long period of relaxation for himself. "Quiet!" he roared. "You heard what I said: one plus two plus three plus and-so-forth, up to two hundred." He continued in a sharp voice, "Now get busy; don't waste any time."

The teacher glanced about the room to check that every head was bent over a slate. Then he leaned back in his arm chair, yawned, settled himself comfortably, and closed his eyes. He took two or three deep, slow breaths, when . . .

"Clack!" He was jarred awake by a sharp report. He brought his eyes into focus, and saw a slate, upside down, resting on his desk. He turned his eyes to see what fool had done this, and there was Carl Friedrich Gauss, a quiet boy of nine, standing by his desk.

Carl Friedrich inclined his head toward his slate. "There it is," he stated simply. The custom was to make a contest of every problem. The first child to get an answer placed his slate, upside down, on the schoolmaster's desk. The next to finish placed his slate, also upside down on top of the first one, and so on. When all the slates were piled up, the whole stack was turned over, and the owner of the first to have the right answer was declared the winner. Carl Friedrich seemed to imply that he had already obtained the answer to this lengthy problem in addition—in just a couple of moments!

Herr Buttner glared directly at the quiet boy. He was interfering with the teacher's rest, a serious matter. If it had been anyone else in the school, Herr Buttner would have been sure that he was either a complete fool, or was being a "wise guy." But Carl Friedrich was neither a fool nor a jokester. In the small town of Braunschweig, stories of unusual events soon became common knowledge, and the teacher had heard of what had happened when Carl Friedrich was four years old: the little boy had been watching his father, a mason contractor, figuring up the weekly wages of his various workmen. Tugging at his father's sleeve, Carl Friedrich had pointed out to him where he had made a mistake in his computation. So there was a slight chance that the boy had devised some shortcut for the problem of adding up the whole numbers from one to two hundred.

On the other hand, Carl Friedrich had appeared to be merely a docile, hard-working pupil in his two years in school, exhibiting no signs of extraordinary talent; and now, at the age of nine, he was just beginning arithmetic—he hadn't had time to learn much from Herr Buttner. In any case, the teacher didn't want to be cheated out of his rest.

"Sit down, boy," he growled. "We'll look at your slate later."

So, Carl Friedrich returned to his bench, folded his

hands, and sat, quiet and thoughtful, while the others struggled with the addition. Occasionally, he smiled to himself as his neighbors muttered when they made mistakes and rubbed them out, as they whispered under their breaths to remind themselves of how much to "carry," and as they sometimes glanced in wonderment at the little boy who had obtained the answer—at least *an* answer—so quickly.

Herr Buttner found that he couldn't enjoy his rest, after his rude awakening, so he went up and down the aisles, exhorting the pupils to hurry, and glaring at the self-confident Carl Friedrich. He probably half-wished that Carl's answer would be incorrect; then he might employ the switch to discipline the boy's impertinence.

Finally, after a long time had passed, another slate was placed on Carl Friedrich's; and, in another ten minutes, half a dozen more were piled on. When most of the slates were in, Herr Buttner went to the desk and turned the pile over. All eyes were on him as he picked up Carl Friedrich's slate, on which a single number was written: 20,100. The teacher recognized this as the correct answer, and gave a nod of acknowledgment to the boy. The other slates were quickly checked: there were some correct answers, but most of the pupils had lost their footings in the morass of addition, and had come up with incorrect values for the sum.

According to report, Herr Buttner soon appreciated the remarkable qualities of Carl Friedrich Gauss, atoning for his early skepticism and sarcasm by sending to the big city of Hamburg for the best arithmetic book available, which the teacher provided from his own meager funds for the boy.

19

JULY 1 AND DECEMBER 25

WILL CUPPY

I suppose, when I stop and think seriously about it, Mr. Cuppy's *How to Get from January to December* is not such a strange place to find mathematicians. After all, they have to be born too. Or do they just assume themselves into existence?

JULY 1

Gottfried Wilhelm Leibnitz, German philosopher and mathematician, was born at Leipzig on July 1, 1646. It is somewhat difficult to say what Leibnitz thought about everything, as he didn't write it all down, but he is generally regarded as a great thinker. A great thinker is one who tells us it isn't so. This provides an endless succession of great thinkers, which is very nice for them but it leaves the rest of us at a rather loose end.

Leibnitz had a lot to do with inventing the differential and the integral calculus, a branch of mathematics the exact nature of which has always eluded me—you have to be that way before you can understand it. He was also fond of talking at some length about what he called *the infinitely little*. One day, after he had tried to explain the infinitely little to Charlotte Sophia, wife of Frederick I of Prussia, she exclaimed to a lady-in-waiting: "Mon Dieu! As if I did not know enough of that!"

P.S. Our philosopher had his practical side too. He presented Peter the Great with a plan for reorganizing Russia's educational system, a main feature being a salary of 500 rubles per year for himself. He didn't get it.

You have heard about Gottfried Wilhelm Leibnitz, and now Mr. Cuppy turns to Sir Isaac Newton, who, many people contend, really invented the calculus. In any event, late in the seventeenth century, there was quite an emotional and unscholarly battle between the followers of Newton and those of Leibnitz, as to who really invented the calculus. My own opinion is that Sir Isaac has a slight edge, since he was born on December 25.

DECEMBER 25

Sir Isaac Newton was one of those persons who lost out on two sets of presents because they were born on Christmas. He arrived in 1642, and I wish I could give you the real facts about that apple. Some say that Sir Isaac did *not* think up his theory of gravitation while watching an apple fall from a tree, and others say that they could show you the very tree from which the apple fell. Apple or no apple, I have always admired the great man's comments on the passing of Roger Cotes, a brilliant young mathematician cut off in his prime in 1716. Said Sir Issac, then nearing seventy-four and as full of honors as one can well be: "If Mr. Cotes had lived, we should have known something." You don't hear Grade B scientists talking like that.

20

A PURE MATHEMATICIAN

ARTHUR GUITERMAN

Mathematicians have long had the reputation of living
in their own world, rather oblivious of what is going
on around them. Of course, today mathematicians are
probably not content to simply "square hypotenuses,"
but the idea's the same.

Mr. Guiterman wrote many books of poetry, several
plays, and the libretto of the opera *A Man Without a
Country* which was produced by the Metropolitan
Opera Company. The books of poetry include *Betel
Nuts, The Laughing Muse,* and *The Mirthful Lyre,*
which titles suggest, to me anyway, real enjoyment
within. Mrs. Guiterman wrote to say that this was one
of her husband's favorite poems, among the many he
wrote. It's one of my favorites too.

Let Poets chant of Clouds and Things
    In lonely attics!
A Nobler Lot is his who clings
    To Mathematics.
Sublime he sits, no Worldly Strife
    His Bosom vexes,
Reducing all the Doubts of Life
    To Y's and X's.
And naught to him's a Primrose on
    The river's border;

89

A Parallelepipedon
  Is more in order.
Let Zealots vow to do and dare
  And right abuses!
He'd rather sit at home and square
  Hypotenuses.
Along his straight-ruled paths, he goes
  Contented with 'em,
The only Rhythm that he knows,
  A Logarithm!

21

A NOTE ON LOGARITHMS
CHARLES F. LINN

In case you haven't run into these things, the name is
the toughest part of them. Actually, they are no more than
exponents—but exponents expressing four and five place
decimals—and are used to simplify calculations. With logarithms, or "logs," as they are more conveniently known,
multiplication is reduced to addition, subtraction gives you
answers to long division problems, finding the square root
is accomplished with simple division by 2 . . . and so on.

Logarithms come in two parts, characteristics and mantissas, but I could never remember whether the character-
istic was the decimal part and the mantissa the whole
number part, or vice versa. Anyway, you find them in
books of tables—"log tables," if you will, and that reminds
me of a story.

It seems that among the pairs of animals that Noah took
with him on the ark, were Mr. and Mrs. Adder. Noah
noticed one day that while all the other animals were
strolling about on the deck with their young, Mr. and Mrs.
Adder were childless. He asked them about this and was
told that since they were adders they could not multiply.

Noah was somewhat surprised, and thought this most
unfortunate, but soon forgot about the incident, as he turned
his hand to the activities related to responsible arksmanship.

One of the things he did during the next few days was to fashion a rather crude table from some driftwood that chanced by the ark. This table was, by chance, placed in the quarters of Mr. and Mrs. Adder.

Sometime later, Noah was surprised to see Mr. and Mrs. Adder promenading on the deck with several small adders. He hurried over to ask them about this. "Oh yes, they are ours, and we're very grateful to you. You provided us with a log table, and now we can multiply."

22

AGHA AND MATH

VLADIMAR KARAPATOFF

The story that follows gives another point of view on the logarithm business. The author, Vladimir Karapatoff, was an electrical engineer, who taught in several Russian colleges and consulted for the Russian government before coming to the United States in 1903. In the United States he served as a consultant for various industries and taught electrical engineering at Cornell University from 1904 to 1939.

Dr. Karapatoff invented and patented several electrical devices, and also a five-stringed cello, which he played in public. He played the piano well enough to give public performances and wrote a book of poetry, *Rhythmical Tales of Stormy Years* (1937).

Once there lived in an oriental country a rich landed proprietor. He had a long string of names—first, middle, and last—each in honor of an ancestor, but to those about him he was simply known as Agha, the Master. He had numerous slaves who raised crops for him, took care of his orchards, and looked after his livestock. Only two out of his wives were living, and among his children there was a pretty girl, Rhia, of marriageable age. In fact, a neighboring landed proprietor, Hussein, wanted to marry her, but he already had five wives which was the maximum number allowed by the law. He had to wait until one of them died or could be disposed of as a present to one of his hangers-on. Of course, he could take her as a harem woman, or, using a Navy expression, wife's mate, Third Class, but Agha was too proud to consent to such an arrangement. The city of Khaleb, situated on a large navigable river, was just half a day's journey from Agha's estate, by oxcart, and his produce and cattle were occasionally taken there for sale on market days.

It was this disposal of his farm products and the buying of spices, silks, and a few other items that were among Agha's principal headaches. He had some faithful slaves and skilled supervisors, but it was difficult to find a man who could keep books, enter the sales and the purchases, and know how to figure out the amount of supplies on hand, and to tell Agha if he was making money, and if so how much.

Now Agha was a thrifty man, in spite of his great wealth, and always insisted on accurate bookkeeping and accounting. For example, if he sent to the market seventeen calves, to be sold at eleven silverpieces each, he wanted to know what the total amount would be. Each of his supervisors and some intelligent slaves always had to carry at their belts leather bags filled with pebbles. In the above case, the slave to be sent with the calves had to put on a table, side by side, seventeen piles of pebbles, eleven pebbles in each pile, and then count the total number of pebbles. As a precaution, another slave was ordered to do the same in a different room, and then each reported his findings to Agha. If there was a discrepancy, each was given ten lashes at the whipping post, and two other slaves were called to do the addition anew, until the amount was settled. Then those who got the right amount (or at least checked each other) had to give twenty lashes to the others. This they were always glad to do, having received undeserved punishment before. This is how the old saying originated: "Accuracy is in your hands, inaccuracy on your back." Later the proverb was abridged to the terse saying: "Inaccuracy hurts." Anyway this problem of correct accounts was on Agha's mind most of the time, and he kept his eye open for an improvement in the situation.

One day Agha had several carts with produce and cattle at the Khaleb market, and he was strolling among the vendors surveying the situation and watching his slaves and other merchants. He noticed a young man, whom he had never seen before, approaching a vendor and after a brief conference taking out a peculiar contraption from a bag, doing something with this contraption, whispering something to the vendor, and then replacing the contraption in the bag. Whereupon the vendor gave the young man a copper coin and the young man thanked him and went to the next vendor. Some accepted his services, others shook their heads negatively. Agha was naturally a curious person, and in this case he wanted to be sure that nothing was being done to put him at a disadvantage in selling his wares. So he followed the young man and finally asked him what he was doing. "Oh," said the young man in a pleasant lisp, "I am Math, the Abacus, and I figure out the amounts of sales for my clients. May I therve you thir? My charges are very reasonable and the accuracy is guaranteed."

"I saw you take a gadget out of that bag and use it. May I see it?" asked Agha.

"Sorry, thir," said Math the Abacus hastily, "this device

is my stock in trade and I keep it partly covered even when I am using it."

"Listen, Math. I am Agha, the well-known landed proprietor up the river and I can make your future if your judgment is as good as your skill is supposed to be. I want to talk to you tonight, over yonder at Mustapha's coffee house. Be there soon after sunset."

Seated over their cups of fragrant Arabian coffee, Agha said to the young man, "First tell me about yourself and how you happen to be in this town."

"My story is very simple," answered Math. "My father is a small landed proprietor a few miles down the river, and of course we all have heard of you, Agha. My father naturally wanted me to stay on his estate since he is getting old and weak. Besides, he wanted me to marry a neighbor's daughter, Podagra, for whom I do not care at all. I am more of a bookworm, and my ambition is to become an astrologer. This is why I ran away from home and came here hoping to enter the Astrologers' Academy in Khaleb. Unfortunately, they want too much money for instruction, and I also have to have something to live on until I am skilled enough in predicting the course of planets and their influence on human fortunes. . . ." The young man stopped and looked at Agha as if to find out if this information was just what he wanted.

"What is your real name?" asked Agha.

"My name is Massy, or Mass for short, but on account of my lisping which you no doubt have noticed, I have to pronounce it Math, and that's how I got this nickname."

"What about the rest of your name—the Abacus?" asked Agha.

"Oh, this is the name of my computing device which has

come from India and is not known in this country. With it I can figure out large amounts in no time—for example, 245 bushels of grain at 31 coppers a bushel. Of course, I had to develop considerable speed in my fingers, and my brain just naturally takes to figures. On market days I am making good money and I am saving as much as I can to pursue my studies at the Astrologers' Academy." Agha looked over the young man carefully, and with his knowledge of human nature he quickly sized up the young man as honest but rather impractical, though intellectual. His clothes were shabby and torn, his countenance emaciated and it was clear that he was barely eking out his existence.

"Here's my proposition to you, Math the Abacus," said Agha. "I am willing to take you on my estate as an indentured servant for two years. You are to live with my other servants and to be treated as such, including occasional floggings for mistakes and knavery. Your duties will be to keep accounts, train others in doing figures, and find out my profit or loss."

"But I cannot disclose the secrets of my abacus," interrupted Math hastily.

"Damn the abacus," said Agha. "My slaves could not understand it anyway, nor could they develop the skill in their horny fingers to handle it. Just make them count the pebbles quickly and accurately. There is no better way of getting practical results."

"Oh, yes there is," said Math, "by multiplication, instead of addition."

"I had a Greek slave once," Agha told him, "who mentioned multiplication to me. I had to flog him three times before he gave up the idea, and I shall do the same to you."

"But Agha," exclaimed Math, "multiplication is used in the Astrologers' Academy in computing paths of celestial bodies, and it is a much quicker method than your addition of pebbles. . . ."

"You heard me," said Agha sternly, "now listen further. For two years you will just get your keep and a few coppers to spend when I send you to town. But if your work is satisfactory and you prove to be a loyal servant, at the end of two years I shall give you three purses of gold. One will pay for your Academy instruction, one will keep your body and soul together while you are learning to fool and deceive people by gazing at the stars, and the third one will start you on your career. Yes or no?"

"I most gratefully accept your offer, merciful Agha," said the young man avidly, "and I am ready to go with you any time you return to your estate."

Thus it was that Math the Abacus became installed on Agha's estate as bookkeeper, accountant, and teacher of addition. In spite of his superior skill in arithmetic, he was modest and patient with the slaves and helped them all he could in their computations, to save them from the whipping post. He himself was careful not to mention multiplication to his master, although he practiced it secretly in arriving at results on his abacus.

This abacus which he carefully concealed from everyone consisted of a set of wooden sticks with ten beads on each stick. Each bead on the first stick is worth one unit; on the second stick each bead is worth ten units; on the third each bead is worth one hundred, etc. When he wanted to add 3 and 4, he moved three beads to the other end of the stick and then four beads more. The result was 7 beads. When he wanted to add 5 and 7, he set off 5 beads and

then he could not set off 7 more, so he added 5 only, re-
stored the 10, took a bead off the next stick which was
worth ten and added 2 more on the first stick, thus getting
a result of 12. Of course, he developed such a dexterity
of fingers in addition and subtraction that no one could
tell by watching his fingers just how he was getting his
results. When it came to multiplication, he quickly converted
it into addition. For example, if someone in the household
wanted to know how much 7 yards of cloth were at 13
coppers per yard, he said to himself, "Three times 7 is 21,"
and marked off 2 and 1 on the adjacent sticks of the abacus.
Then he whispered, "Seven times 10 is 70," and added 7
beads to the previously marked 2. He did all this partly
covering the abacus, working by touch, so no one could
tell what he was doing. Then he would glance at the
beads and say modestly, "I believe it is 91, but you better
check it on your pebbles." It goes without saying that the
addition on pebbles always confirmed his results. Thus in
time all the slaves and supervisors explicitly believed his
computations, and his influence gradually grew, the more
so as he picked up a little astrology here and there and
occasionally predicted rain, the sex of infants about to be
born, or a flogging. When his predictions did not come
true, it was always the case of a hostile planet or con-
stellation which he hadn't noticed in time to correct his
prediction.

A year passed. At first he counted weeks and days
when his indenture would end so he could return to Khaleb
and enter the Astrologers' Academy, but now he seemed to
dread the approach of that day. The simple reason was the
two bright stars on the face of the pretty Rhia which sparkled
every time he happened to meet her in his routine calls

at the master's house. Of course, he belonged to the same class of society as Agha, and from this point of view was entitled to ask for Rhia's hand, but what chance had he, a poor indentured servant who hoped to become an astrologer? Besides, he had learned from other slaves that Rhia was partly promised to the rich Hussein as soon as his heart would become vacant for a new love. Nevertheless, so strong was Math's love that he took the courage to speak to Agha about it in rather general roundabout terms. But the shrewd landowner interrupted him,

"Are you still thinking of that multiplication, or are you now convinced that addition is the only practical way of business bookkeeping, no matter what those faker astrologers of yours believe?"

Now Math remembered the threat of flogging, and he knew that it was either multiplication or Rhia, so he said modestly, "You are my benefactor, and through you I hope to become an independent astrologer. Your servants and overseers are doing well with pebbles under my direction, so why should I invite trouble for myself?"

"But isn't it true," persisted Agha, "that you are using that cursed multiplication on your abacus?"

"I came here under the condition that my abacus and the method of its use should remain my secret," said Math quietly, "and I am sure that my master will want to keep his part of our bargain."

"I do not care how you use that cursed contraption of yours," said Agha, "but when you leave we shall have to go back to our slow addition on pebbles, with constant floggings and cutting out of manti-issas."

Now manti-issa was an article of food that the slaves were particularly fond of, and when a servant obtained a wrong result in counting pebbles, he was not only flogged, but deprived of this important article of food for a few weeks, depending on the magnitude of the error committed. This manti-issa consisted of pig's duodenum stuffed with scraps of meat from the master's table, and was practically the only meat dish that the slaves had. Being deprived of manti-issa (which literally means "filled little stomach") was considered almost as severe a punishment as ten lashes, and this made the slaves doubly careful in counting the pebbles.

"I'll tell you what I have in mind," continued Agha. "Whatever that multiplication is, there ought to be some way of doing the same thing by addition. Of course, I do not know how this is to be achieved, but you are supposed to be skilled at figures, and ought to be able to invent a way."

"Does the master have in mind that if I have to take 13 seven times (which makes 91) I could add two numbers instead and still obtain 91?"

"Something of the sort," said Agha carelessly, rising to his feet.

"But merciful Agha," exclaimed the youth in despair, "it is not humanly possible to add two figures and to obtain the same result as by multiplying them. The only exception is 2 plus 2 and 2 times 2. . . ."

"Very well," said Agha quietly, "I understood you to say, or rather to hint, that you would like me to give you my daughter Rhia in marriage. I hereby consent to this marriage provided that you bring me instructions whereby multiplication (that cursed operation which I do not understand) is replaced by plain addition which anyone can understand. The morning after you demonstrate this trick to my satisfaction Rhia will be yours—and Hussein can keep his five wives."

Math the Abacus was both crushed and excited. The problem still seemed impossible of solution, but now he could think of Rhia at least as of a possible though remote goal, and perhaps speak to her occasionally, and have her encouragement. All he knew so far was that she smiled responsively when she passed by. Now he dared to speak to her and tell her how the thought of her would inspire him to a superhuman effort to accomplish the impossible. Yes, he succeeded in seeing her alone and he told her what her father demanded as the price of her hand, and she told him how her thought would always be with him, and how he should work and have courage, until they would be united.

Now came long sleepless nights of inquiry and search into numbers and their properties. During the day he was fully occupied with the records and computations of all sorts, and there wasn't that quiet solitude which a genius needs for creative work. The first gleam of hope came to him that there existed in arithmetic something akin to what Agha demanded of him, namely, the addition of powers of ten. "One hundred," he said to himself, "is ten to the power of two, and one thousand is ten to the power of three. The product of the two is one hundred thousand, or which is the same, ten to the power of five. Thus to multiply ten to the second power by ten to the third power, we simply added the exponents, that is the powers of ten which represented the two multiplicants."

His logical mind immediately saw the next step. If any number, say 2, could be thought of as a power of ten, then the problem would be solved. What power of 10, 2 was he could not even imagine, so he called it x, and wrote

$10^x=2$. Similarly, he said to himself, we would write $10^y=3$. Here y is the unknown power to which 10 must be raised to obtain 3. Assuming this to be possible, the logical consequence would be:

$$2 \text{ times } 3=10^x \text{ times } 10^y=10^{x+y}=6$$

Thus, instead of multiplying 2 by 3, it is only necessary to add x and y. Then, if we know what power of 10, 6 was we should have our answer. "Maybe the old Agha isn't so dumb as I thought—in fact, he seems to possess a great mathematical intuition."

With renewed vigor and hope he returned to this problem over and over again as the time of his departure for Khaleb grew closer and closer. Now that he could see Rhia occasionally he wanted time to pass as slowly as possible, the more so since he hoped to solve the mathematical task put before him by his master. He now concentrated on the question of what power of 10 the quantity 2 was. He said to himself, "two lies between 1 and 10. Ten to the power of 1 is 10 and 10 to the power of zero is 1. Hence, 2 must be equal to a power of 10 lying between zero and 1." Yet he still could not see any way of finding the value of this power. So he said to himself, "suppose I assume, as the first approximation, that 2 is 10 to the power of 0.2; 3 is 10 to the power of 0.3, etc.; 9 is 10 to the power of 0.9, and finally 10 is 10 to the power of 1." It did not take him long, however, to discover some inconsistencies in these assumptions. For example, 2 times 3 is 6, so that the exponent of 6 should be the sum of those of 2 and 3. Yet, according to his assumption, the sum of these exponents was 0.5, whereas the exponent of 6 was 0.6. Again 3 times 3 is 9, so if the exponent of 3 is 0.3, the exponent of 9 should be 0.6, whereas he assumed it to be equal to 0.9. By several trials of this sort, he concluded that the exponents of 2, 3, etc., were larger than he had assumed. So instead of taking them equal to 0.2, 0.3, etc., he now assumed them to be equal to 0.3, 0.4, etc., and the exponent of 9 to be 0.95, instead of 0.9. New trials showed that the new figures gave products closer to the correct values than before. When this moment came, he at once realized that he was on a fair way toward a solution of Agha's problem which instead of being an absurd supposition of an ignorant man was an intuitive flash of a genius, a flash that would make Math's name go to posterity as that of a prominent mathematician who made complicated computations possible in a simple manner.

After another tete-a-tete with Rhia, he now betook himself to finding more accurate figures for those exponents of the first nine digits. His goal was to find such values of these exponents that any two exponents when added gave the exponent of the number which is the product of these two numbers. After several nights, he finally arrived at the following figures:

Nos.	1	2	3	4	5	6	7	8	9	10
exponents of	0.000	0.301	0.477	0.602	0.699	0.778	0.845	0.903	0.954	1.000

He then realized that he had to extend this table to include the exponents of all the numbers up to 100. At first the task seemed tremendous, but gradually he recognized that he already had the exponents of a goodly number of quantities greater than 10. For example, the exponent of 20 is 1.301, because it had to be equal to the sum of the exponents of 2 and 10. The exponent of 24 is 1.380, for it had to be equal to the sum of the exponents of 8 and 3, or of 4 and 6. Before he knew it, he had the exponents of all but the prime numbers between 10 and 100. These prime numbers, like 29 or 71, were not numerous and he could guess at their exponents from those of the two adjacent numbers.

Finally he was able to record on a piece of sheepskin the exponents of all the numbers between 1 and 100. His devoted Rhia learned to help him, and secretly checked one multiplication after another, until they could find no combination that did not check. For example, she would take the exponents of 8 and 12 and add them. The result would give the exponent of 96, as it should be.

Then it was a matter of more patience and more figuring to extend the table to 1000. On the night Math finished his table, for the first time in many months, he slept the sleep of a man assured of his future, his fame, and a loving wife.

I wish I could report truthfully that he dreamt of beautiful Rhia, but he was too tired to dream of anything or anybody. The shepherd's pipe awakened him before the sunrise. He jumped up; realization of his luck became clear to him suddenly, and he ran to his master's house. He stopped before Agha's bedroom window and began shouting at the top of his shrill voice, lisping more than ever,

"Lo! Agha, Rhia ith mine!"

The master woke and naturally assumed that the house was on fire, until he recognized Math's familiar lisp. He told the woman in attendance that night to call the chief supervisor who slept a few rooms away. When he appeared, Agha instructed him to give Math twenty lashes for disturbing the peace. "Put him on bread and water for a month, and see to it that no manti-issa is slipped to him. After a month I may be willing to hear what he has to say."

Fortunately time was counted in that country by lunar months so that Math's punishment lasted only twenty-eight days instead of thirty. Finally his new system of multiplication by addition was presented to Agha and approved by him as being within the intellectual grasp of the dumbest of his servants and slaves. He received Rhia for his wife and the promised three purses of gold. Hussein was just a day late in palming off one of his wives, but Math arranged for him to marry Podagra, the girl his father wanted him to marry.

That cry, "Lo, Agha, Rhia ith mine," was heard and repeated later all over the estate, the other servants teasing Math with it. He and Rhia had to hear it all day long, repeated with different intonations and even sung to a popular tune. Finally the sentence became contracted to lo-'ga-rhi'th-mi, and so one day, Rhia who was very proud of her husband, suggested that the exponents which he computed be called logarithmi, in honor of that call that brought Math happiness and fame. Later scholars, ignorant of the origin of this name, assumed the final 'i' to be a Latin plural and so it was that for centuries a single exponent became known as the logarithmus. Before presenting his discovery to the Astrologers' Academy, Math wanted a name for the part of the logarithm after the decimal point.

"What was it that you missed the most during those twenty-eight days when you were in the doghouse?" Rhia asked coyly, expecting a sentimental answer.

But Math was truthful, and besides you do not have to be nice to your own wife, so he said, "What I missed the most was those manti-issas, especially when I could smell them from the kitchen."

"All right," said Rhia in an offended tone, "then you are welcome to call the fractional portions of logarithms mantissas, so you will never miss those nasty things again."

And this is how we still refer to mantissas of logarithms.

Moral of the story: "Don't pick out a girl for whom you have to do a lot of arithmetic and algebra. There are plenty of others, just as good, for whom you don't have to lift a finger."

23

QUATRAINS

OMAR KHAYYAM

One of the greatest mathematicians of his time, and, possibly, of all time was the Persian Omar Khayyam. His name actually means Omar the Tentmaker (his father may have been a tentmaker, and possibly Omar himself spun a few before he went on the government payroll).

While some of his mathematical writings survive, Omar is almost universally remembered for his quatrains, in which he made fun of the mystics of his time. Occasionally, however, you can find a reference in a quatrain to matters mathematical.

Ah, but my computations, people say
Have squared the year to human reckoning, nay
If so, by striking from the calendar
Unborn tomorrow and dead yesterday.

Of "Is" and "Is not," though by rule and line
And "Up" and "Down" by logic I define
Of all the things that men should care to fathom
I was never deep in anything but wine.

And if the wine you drink, the lip you press
End in the nothing all things end in, yes
Then fancy while thou art, thou art but what thou shalt be
Nothing. Thou shalt not be less.

24

VISION

GEORGE DAVID BIRKHOFF

George David Birkhoff was one of the great American mathematicians of this century, of all centuries, for that matter. He became interested in making up a formula by which he could measure beauty—beauty in painting, in music, in poetry, and even in vases.

Now this is quite an undertaking, and Professor Birkhoff was the first to admit that his formulas were not adequate. Still, it was an interesting attempt, and you may want to read his book, *Aesthetic Measure*, sometime. When he got around to comparing vases, he designed a few himself, according to his formula. He also wrote a poem which would measure up to his poetry beauty-formula.

Wind and wind the wisps of fire,
Bits of knowledge, hearts desire;
Soon with the central ball
Fiery vision will enthrall.

Wind too long or strip the sphere,
See the vision disappear!

Incidentally, Professor Birkhoff gave "Vision" a .62 rating. He scored "The Raven," which Poe constructed mathematically, a .75.

25

AN UNTITLED POEM FROM IRELAND

WILLIAM ROWAN HAMILTON

You may want to argue that Ireland is really not such a strange place for a mathematician. But, I find a remarkable paucity of Irish mathematicians, so that Sir William Rowan Hamilton does stand out.

Hamilton started off fast, but in languages. By the age of five he was able to read Latin, Greek and Hebrew—the three languages which a learned person of his time (early nineteenth century) was supposed to master. (No mention of Gaelic, though.) At ten he was tackling Arabic and Sanskrit. He had worked at mathematics, beginning at the age of three, but had not really given it serious attention until, at the age of twelve, he met Zerah Colburn, an American boy of about the same age, who was remarkably gifted in mental arithmetic.

This meeting inspired Hamilton to try his hand at the same kind of mental gymnastic. And, from there he went on to advanced mathematics. He achieved an international reputation as a mathematician at the age of seventeen, after finding and correcting an error in one of the most difficult mathematical works.

In between mathematical undertakings, Hamilton wrote some rather remarkable poems which seem to me to reflect his interest in the Persian literature and language. Here's one, apparently never named.

O brooding Spirit of Wisdom and of Love,
Whose mighty wings even now o'ershadow me,
Absorb me in thine own immensity,
And raise me far my finite self above.
Purge vanity away, and the weak care
That name or fame of me may widely spread.
And the deep wick keep burning in their stead,
Thy blissful influence afar to bear—
Or see it borne. Let no desire of ease
No lack of courage, faith, or love, delay
Mine own steps, or that high thought-paven way
In which my soul her dear commission sees.
Yet with an equal joy let me behold
Thy chariot o'er that way by others rolled.

26

THALES MEASURES A PYRAMID

CHARLES F. LINN

You may have read, one place or another, about Euclid's
encounter with an urchin on the steps of the library of
Alexandria. The lad had all kinds of embarrassing questions
to ask the mathematician about his book. But, it seems that
Euclid was not the first Greek mathematician to run into
this problem. Thales, who lived several centuries before
Euclid, tangled with an uninhibited youngster on one of
his trips to Egypt. Of course, all this was before the in-
vention of Little League and Community Recreation Pro-
grams, and all the kids had to do of a summer day was sit
around and ask embarrassing questions of the visiting mathematicians.

Anyway, it seems that friend Thales wandered down to
Egypt one year to see the sights and, incidentally, try to
learn a bit about the very practical work the Egyptians did
in geometry. He became particularly intrigued with the
pyramids and the problem of measuring the height of a pyramid. The direct approach was "out," since even if he
climbed to the tip of the pyramid there was no way of measuring straight down. And, anyway, the Greeks were not
much inclined toward direct approaches when they could
work out a nice mathematical solution. So, Thales sat down
to give the matter some thought.

After a number of weeks spent thinking and calculating,

he thought he had the problem solved, so he gathered up his drawing board, pencils, papyrus and a few instruments he had built, and went out to the pyramid.

Setting up shop there under his beach umbrella, Thales was working busily, when a small boy wandered up. "Whaddarya doin' with all that stuff out in the hot sun?" he asked.

"I'm calculating the height of yonder pyramid," replied Thales.

"Oh," said the boy. "Looks like the hard way."

Thales wasn't really listening to what the boy said, and continued his calculating, muttering to himself. "Hmmm . . . angle of 34 degrees 13 minutes, and 47 seconds . . . arc sine . . . hummm . . . tangent . . . confounded cheap pencils . . . now, where's the table . . . hummmmm . . . multiply by 1.414 . . . drat . . . someone should invent a ball-point pen . . . bah . . . made a mistake somewhere . . ."

About that time the boy interrupted this monologue. "I don't see why you need all these numbers and things."

Thales mumbled on. "Hmmmm, let's see . . . no . . . go away, lad . . . no, wait . . . I'll explain. You see all these numbers are related to the angles—this is a new thing— just invented it. Think I'll call it 'trigonometry.' You see, you get the angle on the top of the pyramid with this instrument here—just invented that too—and then you look up in the table . . . and you measure the distance . . . and . . . drat it, you've got me all confused. Anyway, you measure this distance . . . and then . . . I think . . . you multiply it by this number which is the cosine of the angle . . . No, . . . think I'll call this the 'tangent,' and then you'll have the height of the pyramid . . . drat it . . . something's wrong . . . hmmmm . . . confounded pencils . . ."

"I don't see it at all," the boy observed. "Still looks like the hard way to me."

"Look, kid," Thales broke in sharply. "This trigonometry is a complicated business. Why, I'm inventing a whole new branch of mathematics. This isn't for the likes of you. Now, go away and let me figure . . . hmmm . . . maybe sine of 34 degrees . . . bah . . . that couldn't be right . . ."

The lad was not so easily put off. "But look, Mr. Thales, why don't you just measure the shadow of the pyramid, and you'd be all set."

"What's that about the shadow?" Thales interrupted. "You've gotta have trigonometry for this. Now, go away."

"Okay, okay," said the boy. "Don't be so touchy. But if you measured the shadow, and then measured the shadow of one of your long sticks there . . . and you *can* measure the length of the stick . . . you could figure out the height of the pyramid by a simple proportion—shadow of the pyramid is to the height of the pyramid as the shadow of the stick is to the height of the stick—simple, huh?"

"Hmph," Thales snorted, ". . . a crude method . . . lessee . . . tangent of 34 degrees . . . what did you say, boy? Couldn't be that easy . . . now go away. I've work to do . . ."

So, the lad went off to draw a few diagrams in the sand. And, Thales returned to his calculations and mutterings. Later in the day, however, he was seen out beside the pyramid with a stick stuck in the ground, and his measuring rod on the ground.

Evidently his results impressed the folks back home, for Thales feat of measuring the pyramid is much acclaimed in the history books.

And, trigonometry had to wait a few hundred years or so to be invented.

IT'S
STRANGE MATHEMATICS,
IN PLACES

27

NUMBERS ARE WONDERFUL THINGS!

THOMAS MANN

Seven was the number of the moving stars
    and bearers of command,
And to each belonged a day.
But seven was also and especially
    The Moon's number,
Which makes a path for its brothers
    The Gods there in the sky;
For the number of its quarters are seven days each.
    Sun and Moon were two,
Like everything else in the world
    And like yes and no.
Thus one might group the planets
    As two and five—
And how rightly too, considering the five!
For that number had a wonderful relation to twelve,
    Seeing that five times twelve make sixty
    Already known to be sacred;
But even more wonderful with seven,
    For five and seven make twelve.
And that was not all.
For by such division and grouping
    One got a five-day planetary week,
    Of which seventy-two came in the year.

But five was the number by which one must multiply two
   and seventy
     To arrive at the glorious
     Three hundred and sixty—
And this was at once the sum
     Of the days in the year
And the result of that division
     Of the sun's course
By the longest line which could be drawn upon the disc.
How wonderful that was!

28

LIMERICKS

You can find, or invent, a limerick for most any occasion. Here are a few about matters mathematical . . . the first two having, evidently, a common problem in mind.

There was a young fellow from Trinity
Who found the cube root of Infinity
But it gave him such fidgits
To add up the digits
He chucked math and took up divinity

Once a bright young lady called Lillian
Summed the numbers from one to a billion
But it gave her the "fidgits"
To add up the digits
If you can help her, she'll thank you a million

29

WITH WORDS A BIT GARBLED

OGDEN NASH

Ogden Nash can be depended upon to invent new words when he needs them for a rhyme, or slightly modify old words, for the same purpose. He even gets a mathematical word in now and then. Did you notice, for example, in *The Christmas That Almost Wasn't* . . .

Good Oldwin, king of Lullapat
Although not absolutely fat
Might be described as circular.
Delicious dishes did he dip in
Which left rounded like a pippin.
His shape was pippendicular.

30

MOTHER GOOSE MATHEMATICS

You've seen how Mary, Mary quite contrary got into the algebra books. Here's another familiar character in an unfamiliar setting:

Little Jack Horner
Sat in a corner
Extracting cube roots to infinity.
This occupation for boys
Reduces the noise
And makes for a quiet
Vicinity.

Can you top this one?

Old King Cole
Was a merry old soul
Who loved geometry.
Those triangles, he said
Just go to my head.
They suit me to a "T".

31

THE MAJOR GENERAL

W. S. GILBERT

Back a hundred years, when war was still considered something of a gentlemanly sport, a man to be considered "the very model of a modern major general" would want to convince you that he knew something about everything. And, that would, of course, include mathematics. So, you'll find the lines in the Gilbert and Sullivan operetta, *The Pirates of Penzance*.

I'm very well acquainted too
With matters mathematical.
I know about equations
Both the simple and quadratical.
About the binomial theorem
I am teeming with a lot of news
With many cheerful facts
About the square of the hypotenuse.

32

PARABOLA

HOOPER REYNOLDS GOODWIN

This curve I'm plotting? A parabola.
This point is called the focus; it's the point—
Oh, no, not an ellipse. Ellipses have two foci:
Here, I'll show you one I've drawn.
You see the difference. These two lines of the parabola,
They stretch out wide and wider,
"World without end," as preachers say.
(I don't know what they mean; perhaps *they* don't);
But you see how it goes.

There was a man—Sir Isaac Newton, I believe it was—
Who had the notion a parabola was an ellipse,
Its other focus at infinity.
You may not understand just what he meant;
You have to sort of take the thing on faith.
The keenest scholar can't quite picture it, you know.

I've often thought,
It might be called a symbol of man's life;
A curve of ever-widening sweep.
And here in this world
Is the focus we may call, say, temporal interests,
Food and drink and clothes . . .
But yet it cannot be that this is all;

For out beyond the reach of sight must be
Another point, a heavenly focus, see?
'Round which the sweeping curves of human life
Complete the ellipse.
Fantastic? Well, perhaps,
But yet the more I think of it . . .

And here—
Another thing I've often thought about:
Suppose we draw here two parabolas
With axes parallel, and let the arms cross—
"Intersect" the word is—at this point.
Now if there be a focus
Somewhere out beyond the bounds of space,
And these are two ellipses,
As Sir Isaac thought they were,
Why, don't you see, they'll intersect again
Somewhere out there.
Just as two lives that once have crossed,
Then gone their separate ways,
And one has disappeared long since into the void of death
May—but who knows? It's just a thought. . . .

Well, come again; I don't get callers often.
They don't see much in old folks nowadays,
And when a man's not only old, but got his head
Stuck always in a book of "Analyt!"
Young people think I'm queer; they can't see why
A man that doesn't have to study graphs
Should plague his head; don't understand that such
Dry, dull things as a parabolic curve
May bring up mem'ries of a face that's gone.

33

A FINAL WORD

PLATO

Above all, arithmetic
stirs up him who is by
nature sleepy and dull
and makes him quick to
learn, retentive, shrewd
and aided by the art
divine, makes progress
beyond his natural powers.

ABOUT THE AUTHOR

CHARLES F. LINN, the author of ODD ANGLES, was born in Pennsylvania. A graduate of Colgate, he later went to Wesleyan University in Connecticut, where he earned a Master's Degree and, along the way, learned, as he says, "my first insights into what math is all about, and the idea that everyone can be creative in math at his own level."

Mr. Linn not only taught mathematics in public schools, but later was the mathematics editor and writer for two nationally circulated classroom science newspapers. He is currently teaching at Oswego State College in upper New York, and owns a two hundred-year-old summer house on Turkey Hill Road in Haddam, Connecticut. It is at this retreat that he has written his previous books—a mathematics textbook, several mathematics pamphlets, a four-volume history of mathematics series and *Puzzles, Patterns and Pastimes*. In spite of his full work load, he still finds time every year for the celebration of Susan B. Anthony's birthday and the commemoration of the crossing of the River Boyne by King William.